Labor Law

Selected Statutes, Forms, and Agreements

In Memory of our Father & Grandfather:

Steven D. Ostrowsky

Given By:

Your loving family, Sheryl, Denis, Cassidy & Ashley Pearson

2003

Labor Law

Selected Statutes, Forms, and Agreements

Michael C. Harper
Professor of Law
Boston University

Samuel Estreicher
Professor of Law
New York University

Joan Flynn
Associate Professor of Law
Cleveland State University

ASPEN
PUBLISHERS

1185 Avenue of the Americas, New York, NY 10036
www.aspenpublishers.com

Permissions
Aspen Publishers
1185 Avenue of the Americas
New York, NY 10036

Printed in the United States of America

1 2 3 4 5 6 7 8 9 0

ISBN 0-7355-4438-7

About Aspen Publishers

Aspen Publishers, headquartered in New York City, is a leading information provider for attorneys, business professionals, and law students. Written by preeminent authorities, our products consist of analytical and practical information covering both U.S. and international topics. We publish in the full range of formats, including updated manuals, books, periodicals, CDs, and online products.

Our proprietary content is complemented by 2,500 legal databases, containing over 11 million documents, available through our Loislaw division. Aspen Publishers also offers a wide range of topical legal and business databases linked to Loislaw's primary material. Our mission is to provide accurate, timely, and authoritative content in easily accessible formats, supported by unmatched customer care.

To order any Aspen Publishers title, go to *www.aspenpublishers.com* or call 1-800-638-8437.

To reinstate your manual update service, call 1-800-638-8437.

For more information on Loislaw products, go to *www.loislaw.com* or call 1-800-364-2512.

For Customer Care issues, e-mail *CustomerCare@aspenpublishers.com*; call 1-800-234-1660; or fax 1-800-901-9075.

Aspen Publishers
A Wolters Kluwer Company

Contents

Labor Law

**Selected Statutes, Forms,
and Agreements**

Selected Statutes[*]

Sherman Act — Selected Provisions
26 Stat. 209 (1890), as amended, 15 U.S.C. §§1 et seq.

§1. (§1) Trusts, etc., in restraint of trade illegal; penalty

Every contract, combination in the form of trust or otherwise, or conspiracy, in restraint of trade or commerce among the several States, or with foreign nations, is declared to be illegal. Every person who shall make any contract or engage in any combination or conspiracy hereby declared to be illegal shall be deemed guilty of a felony, and, on conviction thereof, shall be punished by fine not exceeding $10,000,000 if a corporation, or, if any other person, $350,000, or by imprisonment not exceeding three years, or by both said punishments, in the discretion of the court.

§2. (§2) Monopolizing trade a felony; penalty

Every person who shall monopolize, or attempt to monopolize, or combine or conspire with any other person or persons, to monopolize any part of the trade or commerce among the several States, or with foreign nations, shall be deemed guilty of a felony, and, on conviction thereof, shall be punished by fine not exceeding $10,000,000 if a corporation, or, if any other person, $350,000, or by imprisonment not exceeding three years, or by both said punishments, in the discretion of the court.

---

[*]The section numbers of the statute involved, as originally enacted, are followed (in parentheses) by the corresponding section numbers in the United States Code (2000 ed.) where appropriate.—EDS.

§4. (§4) Jurisdiction of courts; duty of United States attorneys; procedure

The several district courts of the United States are invested with jurisdiction to prevent and restrain violations of sections 1 to 7 of this title; and it shall be the duty of the several United States attorneys, in their respective districts, under the direction of the Attorney General, to institute proceedings in equity to prevent and restrain such violations. Such proceedings may be by way of petition setting forth the case and praying that such violation shall be enjoined or otherwise prohibited. When the parties complained of shall have been duly notified of such petition the court shall proceed, as soon as may be, to the hearing and determination of the case; and pending such petition and before final decree, the court may at any time make such temporary restraining order or prohibition as shall be deemed just in the premises.

§8. (§7) "Person" defined

The word "person", or "persons", wherever used in sections 1 to 7 of this title shall be deemed to include corporations and associations existing under or authorized by the laws of either the United States, the laws of any of the Territories, the laws of any State, or the laws of any foreign country.

> **Clayton Act — Selected Provisions**
> *38 Stat. 730 (1914), as amended, 15 U.S.C. §§12 et seq.*

§1. (§12) Words defined; short title

(a) "Antitrust laws", as used herein, includes the Act entitled "An Act to protect trade and commerce against unlawful restraints and monopolies", approved July second, eighteen hundred and ninety [Sherman Act, supra]. . . .

(b) This Act may be cited as the "Clayton Act".

§4. (§15) Suits by persons injured

[A]ny person who shall be injured in his business or property by reason of anything forbidden in the antitrust laws may sue therefor in any district court of the United States in the district in which the defendant resides or is found or has an agent, without regard to the amount in controversy, and shall recover threefold the damages by him sustained, and the cost of the suit, including a reasonable attorney's fee. . . .

§6. (§17) Antitrust laws not applicable to labor organizations

The labor of a human being is not a commodity or article of commerce. Nothing contained in the antitrust laws shall be construed to forbid the existence and operation of labor, agricultural, or horticultural organizations, instituted for the purposes of mutual help, and not having capital stock or conducted for profit, or to forbid or restrain individual members of such organizations from lawfully carrying out the legitimate objects thereof; nor shall such organizations, or the members thereof, be held or construed to be illegal combinations or conspiracies in restraint of trade, under the antitrust laws.

§16. (§26) Injunctive relief for private parties; exception; costs

Any person, firm, corporation, or association shall be entitled to sue for and have injunctive relief, in any court of the United States having jurisdiction over the parties, against threatened loss or damage by a violation of the antitrust laws, . . . when and under the same conditions and principles as injunctive relief against threatened conduct that will cause loss or damage is granted by courts of equity, under the rules governing such proceedings, and upon the execution of proper bond against damages for an injunction improvidently granted and a showing that the danger of irreparable loss or damage is immediate, a preliminary injunction may issue. . . . In any action under this section in which the plaintiff substantially prevails, the court shall award the cost of suit, including a reasonable attorney's fee, to such plaintiff.

§20. (§52) Statutory restriction of injunctive relief

No restraining order or injunction shall be granted by any court of the United States, or a judge or the judges thereof, in any case between an employer and employees, or between employers and employees, or between employees, or between persons employed and persons seeking employment, involving, or growing out of, a dispute concerning terms or conditions of employment, unless necessary to prevent irreparable injury to property, or to a property right, of the party making the application, for which injury there is no adequate remedy at law, and such property or property right must be described with particularity in the application, which must be in writing and sworn to by the applicant or by his agent or attorney.

And no such restraining order or injunction shall prohibit any person or persons, whether singly or in concert, from terminating any relation of employment, or from ceasing to perform any work or labor, or from recommending, advising, or persuading others by peaceful means so to do; or from attending at any place where any such person or persons may lawfully be, for the purpose of peacefully obtaining or communicating information, or from peacefully persuading any person to work or to abstain from working; or from ceasing to patronize or to employ any party to such dispute, or from recommending, advising, or persuading others by peaceful and lawful means so to do; or from paying or giving to, or withholding from, any person engaged in such dispute, any strike benefits or other moneys or things of value; or from peaceably assembling in a lawful manner, and for lawful purposes; or from doing any act or thing which might lawfully be done in the absence of such dispute by any party thereto; nor shall any of the acts specified in this paragraph be considered or held to be violations of any law of the United States.

Railway Labor Act of 1926
44 Stat. 577 (1926), as amended, 45 U.S.C. §§151-188

SUBCHAPTER I.   GENERAL PROVISIONS

§1. (§151) Definitions; short title

When used in this chapter and for the purposes of this chapter —

First. The term "carrier" includes any express company, sleeping-car company, carrier by railroad, subject to subtitle IV of Title 49, and any company which is directly or indirectly owned or controlled by or under common control with any carrier by railroad and which operates any equipment or facilities or performs any service (other than trucking service) in connection with the transportation, receipt, delivery, elevation, transfer in transit, refrigeration or icing, storage, and handling of property transported by railroad, and any receiver, trustee, or other individual or body, judicial or otherwise, when in the possession of the business of any such "carrier": *Provided, however,* That the term "carrier" shall not include any street, interurban, or suburban electric railway, unless such railway is operating as a part of a general steam-railroad system of transportation, but shall not exclude any part of the general steam-railroad system of transportation now or hereafter operated by any other motive power. The Interstate Commerce Commission is authorized and directed upon request of the Mediation Board or upon complaint of any party interested to determine after hearing whether any line operated by electric power falls within the terms of this proviso. The term "carrier" shall not include any company by reason of its being engaged in the mining of coal, the supplying of coal to a carrier where delivery is not beyond the mine tipple, and the operation of equipment or facilities therefor, or in any of such activities.

Second. The term "Adjustment Board" means the National Railroad Adjustment Board created by this chapter.

Third. The term "Mediation Board" means the National Mediation Board created by this chapter.

Fourth. The term "commerce" means commerce among the several States or between any State, Territory, or the District of Columbia and any foreign nation, or between any Territory or the District of Columbia and any State, or between any Territory and any other Territory, or between any Territory and the District of Columbia, or within any Territory or the District of Columbia, or between points in the same State but through any other State or any Territory or the District of Columbia or any foreign nation.

Fifth. The term "employee" as used herein includes every person in the service of a carrier (subject to its continuing authority to supervise and direct the manner of rendition of his service) who performs any work defined as that of an employee or subordinate official in the orders of the Interstate Commerce Commission now in effect, and as the same may be amended or interpreted by orders hereafter entered by the Commission pursuant to the authority which is conferred upon it to enter orders amending or interpreting such existing orders: *Provided, however,* That no occupational classification made by order of the Interstate Commerce Commission shall be construed to define the crafts according to which railway employees may be organized by their voluntary action, nor shall the jurisdiction or powers of such employee organizations be regarded as in any way limited or defined by the provisions of this chapter or by the orders of the Commission.

The term "employee" shall not include any individual while such individual is engaged in the physical operations consisting of the mining of coal, the preparation of coal, the handling (other than movement by rail with standard railroad locomotives) of coal not beyond the mine tipple, or the loading of coal at the tipple.

Sixth. The term "representative" means any person or persons, labor union, organization, or corporation designated either by a carrier or group of carriers or by its or their employees, to act for it or them.

Seventh. The term "district court" includes the United States District Court for the District of Columbia; and the term "court of appeals" includes the United States Court of Appeals for the District of Columbia.

This chapter may be cited as the "Railway Labor Act."

§2. (§151a) General purposes

The purposes of the chapter are: (1) To avoid any interruption to commerce or to the operation of any carrier engaged therein; (2) to forbid any limitation upon freedom of association among employees or any denial, as a condition of employment or otherwise, of the right of employees to join a labor organization; (3) to provide for the complete independence of carriers and of employees in the matter of self-organization to carry out the purposes of this chapter; (4) to provide for the prompt and orderly settlement of all disputes concerning rates of pay, rules, or working conditions; (5) to provide for the prompt and orderly settlement of all disputes growing out of grievances or out of the interpretation or application of agreements covering rates of pay, rules, or working conditions.

§2. (§152) General duties

First. Duty of carriers and employees to settle disputes

It shall be the duty of all carriers, their officers, agents, and employees to exert every reasonable effort to make and maintain agreements concerning rates of pay, rules, and working conditions, and to settle all disputes, whether arising out of the application of such agreements or otherwise, in order to avoid any interruption to commerce or to the operation of any carrier growing out of any dispute between the carrier and the employees thereof.

Second. Consideration of disputes by representatives

All disputes between a carrier or carriers and its or their employees shall be considered, and, if possible, decided, with all expedition, in conference between representatives designated and authorized so to confer, respectively, by the carrier or carriers and by the employees thereof interested in the dispute.

Third. Designation of representatives

Representatives, for the purposes of this chapter, shall be designated by the respective parties without interference, influence, or coercion by either party over the designation of representatives by the other; and neither party shall in any way interfere with, influence, or coerce the other in its choice of representatives. Representatives of employees for the purposes of this chapter need not be persons in the employ of the carrier, and no carrier shall, by interference, influence, or coercion seek in any manner to prevent the designation by its employees as their representatives of those who or which are not employees of the carrier.

Fourth. Organization and collective bargaining; freedom from interference by carrier; assistance in organizing or maintaining organization by carrier forbidden; deduction of dues from wages forbidden

Employees shall have the right to organize and bargain collectively through representatives of their own choosing. The majority of any craft or class of employees shall have the right to determine who shall be the representative of the craft or class for the purposes of this chapter. No carrier, its officers, or agents shall deny or in any way question the right of its employees to join, organize, or assist in organizing the labor organization of their choice, and it shall be unlawful for any carrier to interfere in any way with the organization of its employees, or to use the funds of the carrier in maintaining or assisting or contributing to any labor organization, labor representative, or other agency of collective bargaining, or in performing any work therefor, or to influence or coerce employees in an effort to induce them to join or remain or not to join or remain members of any labor organization, or to deduct from the wages of employees any dues, fees, assessments, or other contributions payable to labor organizations, or to collect or to assist in the collection of any such dues, fees, assessments, or other contributions: *Provided*, That nothing in this chapter shall be construed to prohibit a carrier from permitting an employee, individually, or local representatives of employees from conferring with management during working hours without loss of time, or to prohibit a carrier from furnishing free transportation to its employees while engaged in the business of a labor organization.

Fifth. Agreements to join or not to join labor organizations forbidden

No carrier, its officers, or agents shall require any person seeking employment to sign any contract or agreement promising to join or not to join a labor organization; and if any such contract has been enforced prior to the effective date of this chapter, then such carrier shall notify the employees by an appropriate order that such contract has been discarded and is no longer binding on them in any way.

Sixth. Conference of representatives; time; place; private agreements

In case of a dispute between a carrier or carriers and its or their employees, arising out of grievances or out of the interpretation or application of agreements concerning rates of pay, rules, or working conditions, it shall be the duty of the designated representative or representatives of such carrier or carriers and of such employees, within ten days after the receipt of notice of a desire on the part of either party to confer in respect to such dispute, to specify a time and place at which such conference shall be held: *Provided,* (1) That the place so specified shall be situated upon the line of the carrier involved or as otherwise mutually agreed upon; and (2) that the time so specified shall allow the designated conferees reasonable opportunity to reach such place of conference, but shall not exceed twenty days from the receipt of such notice: *And provided further,* That nothing in this chapter shall be construed to supersede the provisions of any agreement (as to conferences) then in effect between the parties.

Seventh. Change in pay, rules, or working conditions contrary to agreement or to section 156 forbidden

No carrier, its officers, or agents shall change the rates of pay, rules, or working conditions of its employees, as a class, as embodied in agreements except in the manner prescribed in such agreements or in section 156 of this title.

Eighth. Notices of manner of settlement of disputes; posting

Every carrier shall notify its employees by printed notices in such form and posted at such times and places as shall be specified by the Mediation Board that all disputes between the carrier and its employees will be handled in accordance with the requirements of this chapter, and in such notices there shall be printed verbatim, in large type, the third, fourth, and fifth paragraphs of this section. The provisions of said paragraphs are made a part of the contract of employment between the carrier and each employee, and shall be held binding upon the parties, regardless of any other express or implied agreements between them.

Ninth. Disputes as to identity of representatives; designation by Mediation Board; secret elections

If any dispute shall arise among a carrier's employees as to who are the representatives of such employees designated and authorized in accordance with the requirements of this chapter, it shall be the duty of the Mediation Board, upon request of either party to the dispute, to investigate such dispute and to certify to both parties, in writing, within thirty days after the receipt of the invocation of its services, the name or names of the individuals or organizations that have been designated and authorized to represent the employees involved in the dispute, and certify the same to the carrier. Upon receipt of such certification the carrier shall treat with the representative so certified as the representative of the craft or class for the purposes of this chapter. In such an investigation, the Mediation Board shall be authorized to take a secret ballot of the employees involved, or to utilize any other appropriate method of ascertaining the names of their duly designated and authorized representatives in such manner as shall insure the choice of representatives by the employees without interference, influence, or coercion exercised by the carrier. In the conduct of any election for the purposes herein indicated the Board shall designate who may participate in the election and establish the rules to govern the election, or may appoint a committee of three neutral persons who after hearing shall within ten days designate the employees who may participate in the election. The Board shall have access to and have power to make copies of the books and records of the carriers to obtain and utilize such information as may be deemed necessary by it to carry out the purposes and provisions of this paragraph.

Tenth. Violations; prosecution and penalties

The willful failure or refusal of any carrier, its officers or agents, to comply with the terms of the third, fourth, fifth, seventh, or eighth paragraph of this section shall be a misdemeanor, and upon conviction thereof the carrier, officer, or agent offending shall be subject to a fine of not less than $1,000, nor more than $20,000, or imprisonment for not more than six months, or both fine and imprisonment, for each offense, and each day during which such carrier, officer, or agent shall willfully fail or refuse to comply with the terms of the said paragraphs of this section shall constitute a separate offense. It shall be the duty of any United States attorney to whom any duly designated representative of a carrier's employees may apply to institute in the proper court and to prosecute under the direction of the Attorney General of the United States, all necessary proceedings for the enforcement of the provisions of this section, and for the punishment of all violations thereof and the costs and expenses of such prosecution shall be paid out of the appropriation for the expenses of the courts of the United States: *Provided,* That nothing in this chapter shall be construed to require an individual employee to render labor or service without his consent, nor shall anything in this chapter be construed to make the quitting of his labor by an individual employee an illegal act; nor shall any court issue any process to compel the performance by an individual employee of such labor or service, without his consent.

Eleventh. Union security agreements; check-off

Notwithstanding any other provisions of this chapter, or of any other statute or law of the United States, or Territory thereof, or of any State, any carrier or carriers as defined in this chapter and a labor organization or labor organizations duly designated and authorized to represent employees in accordance with the requirements of this chapter shall be permitted —

(a) to make agreements, requiring, as a condition of continued employment, that within sixty days following the beginning of such employment, or the effective date of such agreements, whichever is the later, all employees shall become members of the labor organization representing their craft or class: *Provided,* That no such agreement shall require such condition of employment with respect to employees to whom membership is not available upon the same terms and conditions as are generally applicable to any other member or with respect to employees to whom membership was denied or terminated for any reason other than the failure of the employee to tender the periodic dues, initiation fees, and assessments (not including fines and penalties) uniformly required as a condition of acquiring or retaining membership.

(b) to make agreements providing for the deduction by such carrier or carriers from the wages of its or their employees in a craft or class and payment to the labor organization representing the craft or class of such employees, of any periodic dues, initiation fees, and assessments (not including fines and penalties) uniformly required as a condition of acquiring or retaining membership: *Provided,* That no such agreement shall be effective with respect to any individual employee until he shall have furnished the employer with a written assignment to the labor organization of such membership dues, initiation fees, and assessments, which shall be revocable in writing after the expiration of one year or upon the termination date of the applicable collective agreement, whichever occurs sooner.

(c) The requirement of membership in a labor organization in an agreement made pursuant to subparagraph (a) of this paragraph shall be satisfied, as to both a present or future employee in engine, train, yard, or hostling service, that is, an employee engaged in any of the services or capacities covered in the First division of paragraph (h) of section 153 of this title defining the jurisdictional scope of the First Division of the National Railroad Adjustment Board, if said employee shall hold or acquire membership in any one of the labor organizations, national in scope, organized in accordance with this chapter and admitting to membership employees of a craft or class in any of said services; and no agreement made pursuant to subparagraph (b) of this paragraph shall provide for deductions from his wages for periodic dues, initiation fees, or assessments payable to any labor organization other than that in which he holds membership: *Provided, however,* That as to an employee in any of said services on a particular carrier at the effective date of any such agreement on a carrier, who is not a member of any one of the labor organizations, national in scope, organized in accordance with this chapter and admitting to membership employees of a craft or class in any of said services, such employee, as a condition of continuing his employment, may be required to become a member of the organization representing the craft in which he is employed on the effective date of the first agreement applicable to him: *Provided, further,* That nothing herein or in any such agreement or agreements shall prevent an employee from changing membership from one organization to another organization admitting to membership employees of a craft or class in any of said services.

(d) Any provisions in paragraphs Fourth and Fifth of this section in conflict herewith are to the extent of such conflict amended.

§3. (§153) National Railroad Adjustment Board

First. Establishment; composition; powers and duties; divisions; hearings and awards; judicial review

There is established a Board, to be known as the "National Railroad Adjustment Board", the members of which shall be selected within thirty days after June 21, 1934, and it is provided —

(a) That the said Adjustment Board shall consist of thirty-four members, seventeen of whom shall be selected by the carriers and seventeen by such labor organizations of the employees, national in scope, as have been or may be organized in accordance with the provisions of sections 151a and 152 of this title.

(b) The carriers, acting each through its board of directors or its receiver or receivers, trustee or trustees, or through an officer or officers designated for that purpose by such board, trustee or trustees, or receiver or receivers, shall prescribe the rules under which its representatives shall be selected and shall select the representatives of the carriers on the Adjustment Board and designate the division on which each such representative shall serve, but no carrier or system of carriers shall have more than one voting representative on any division of the Board.

(c) Except as provided in the second paragraph of subsection (h) of this section, the national labor organizations, as defined in paragraph (a) of this section, acting each through the chief executive or other medium designated by the organization or association thereof, shall prescribe the rules under which the labor members of the Adjustment Board shall be selected and shall select such members and designate the division on which each member shall serve; but no labor organization shall have more than one voting representative on any division of the Board.

(d) In case of a permanent or temporary vacancy on the Adjustment Board, the vacancy shall be filled by selection in the same manner as in the original selection.

(e) If either the carriers or the labor organizations of the employees fail to select and designate representatives to the Adjustment Board, as provided in paragraphs (b) and (c) of this section, respectively, within sixty days after June 21, 1934, in case of any original appointment to office of a member of the Adjustment Board, or in case of a vacancy in any such office within thirty days after such vacancy occurs, the Mediation Board shall thereupon directly make the appointment and shall select an individual associated in interest with the carriers or the group of labor organizations of employees, whichever he is to represent.

(f) In the event a dispute arises as to the right of any national labor organization to participate as per paragraph (c) of this section in the selection and designation of the labor members of the Adjustment Board, the Secretary of Labor shall investigate the claim of such labor organization to participate, and if such claim in the judgment of the Secretary of Labor has merit, the Secretary shall notify the Mediation Board accordingly, and within ten days after receipt of such advice the Mediation Board shall request those national labor organizations duly qualified as per paragraph (c) of this section to participate in the selection and designation of the labor members of the Adjustment Board to select a representative. Such representative, together with a representative likewise designated by the claimant, and a third or neutral party designated by the Mediation Board, constituting a board of three, shall within thirty days after the appointment of the neutral member, investigate the claims of the labor organization desiring participation and decide whether or not it was organized in accordance with sections 151a and 152 of this title and is otherwise properly qualified to participate in the selection of the labor members of the Adjustment Board, and the findings of such boards of three shall be final and binding.

(g) Each member of the Adjustment Board shall be compensated by the party or parties he is to represent. Each third or neutral party selected under the provisions of paragraph (f) of this section shall receive from the Mediation Board such compensation as the Mediation Board may fix, together with his necessary traveling expenses and expenses actually incurred for subsistence, or per diem allowance in lieu thereof, subject to the provisions of law applicable thereto, while serving as such third or neutral party.

(h) The said Adjustment Board shall be composed of four divisions, whose proceedings shall be independent of one another, and the said divisions as well as the number of their members shall be as follows:

First division: To have jurisdiction over disputes involving train- and yard-service employees of carriers; that is, engineers, firemen, hostlers, and outside hostler helpers, conductors, trainmen, and yard-service employees. This division shall consist of eight members, four of whom shall be selected and designated by the carriers and four of whom shall be selected and designated by the labor organizations, national in scope and organized in accordance with sections 151a and 152 of this title and which represent employees in engine, train, yard, or hostling service: *Provided, however,* That each labor organization shall select and designate two members on the First Division and that no labor organization shall have more than one vote in any proceedings of the First Division or in the adoption of any award with respect to any dispute submitted to the First Division: *Provided further,* however, That the carrier members of the First Division shall cast no more than two votes in any proceedings of the division or in the adoption of any award with respect to any dispute submitted to the First Division.

Second division: To have jurisdiction over disputes involving machinists, boilermakers, blacksmiths, sheet-metal workers, electrical workers, carmen, the helpers and apprentices of all the foregoing, coach cleaners, power-house employees, and railroad-shop laborers. This division shall consist of ten members, five of whom shall be selected by the carriers and five by the national labor organizations of the employees.

Third division: To have jurisdiction over disputes involving station, tower, and telegraph employees, train dispatchers, maintenance-of-way men, clerical employees, freight handlers, express, station, and store employees, signal men, sleeping-car conductors, sleeping-car porters, and maids and dining-car employees. This division shall consist of ten members, five of whom shall be selected by the carriers and five by the national labor organizations of employees.

Fourth division: To have jurisdiction over disputes involving employees of carriers directly or indirectly engaged in transportation of passengers or property by water, and all other employees of carriers over which jurisdiction is not given to the first, second, and third divisions. This division shall consist of six members, three of whom shall be selected by the carriers and three by the national labor organizations of the employees.

(i) The disputes between an employee or group of employees and a carrier or carriers growing out of grievances or out of the interpretation or application of agreements concerning rates of pay, rules, or working conditions, including cases pending and unadjusted on June 21, 1934, shall be handled in the usual manner up to and including the chief operating officer of the carrier designated to handle such disputes; but, failing to reach an adjustment in this manner, the disputes may be referred by petition of the parties or by either party to the appropriate division of the Adjustment Board with a full statement of the facts and all supporting data bearing upon the disputes.

(j) Parties may be heard either in person, by counsel, or by other representatives, as they may respectively elect, and the several divisions of the Adjustment Board shall give due notice of all hearings to the employee or employees and the carrier or carriers involved in any disputes submitted to them.

(k) Any division of the Adjustment Board shall have authority to empower two or more of its members to conduct hearings and make findings upon disputes, when properly submitted, at any place designated by the division: *Provided, however,* That except as provided in paragraph (h) of this section, final awards as to any such dispute must be made by the entire division as hereinafter provided.

(*l*) Upon failure of any division to agree upon an award because of a deadlock or inability to secure a majority vote of the division members, as provided in paragraph (n) of this section, then such division shall forthwith agree upon and select a neutral person, to be known as "referee", to sit with the division as a member thereof, and make an award. Should the division fail to agree upon and select a referee within ten days of the date of the deadlock or inability to secure a majority vote, then the division, or any member thereof, or the parties or either party to the dispute may certify that fact to the Mediation Board, which Board shall, within ten days from the date of receiving such certificate, select and name the referee to sit with the division as a member thereof and make an award. The Mediation Board shall be bound by the same provisions in the appointment of these neutral referees as are provided elsewhere in this chapter for the appointment of arbitrators and shall fix and pay the compensation of such referees.

(m) The awards of the several divisions of the Adjustment Board shall be stated in writing. A copy of the awards shall be furnished to the respective parties to the controversy, and the awards shall be final and binding upon both parties to the dispute. In case a dispute arises involving an interpretation of the award, the division of the Board upon request of either party shall interpret the award in the light of the dispute.

(n) A majority vote of all members of the division of the Adjustment Board eligible to vote shall be competent to make an award with respect to any dispute submitted to it.

(o) In case of an award by any division of the Adjustment Board in favor of petitioner, the division of the Board shall make an order, directed to the carrier, to make the award effective and, if the award includes a requirement for the payment of money, to pay to the employee the sum to which he is entitled under the award on or before a day named. In the event any division determines that an award favorable to the petitioner should not be made in any dispute referred to it, the division shall make an order to the petitioner stating such determination.

(p) If a carrier does not comply with an order of a division of the Adjustment Board within the time limit in such order, the petitioner, or any person for whose benefit such order was made, may file in the District Court of the United States for the district in which he resides or in which is located the principal operating office of the carrier, or through which the carrier operates, a petition setting forth briefly the causes for which he claims relief, and the order of the division of the Adjustment Board in the premises. Such suit in the District Court of the United States shall proceed in all respects as other civil suits, except that on the trial of such suit the findings and order of the division of the Adjustment Board shall be conclusive on the parties, and except that the petitioner shall not be liable for costs in the district court nor for costs at any subsequent stage of the proceedings, unless they accrue upon his appeal, and such costs shall be paid out of the appropriation for the expenses of the courts of the United States. If the petitioner shall finally prevail he shall be allowed a reasonable attorney's fee, to be taxed and collected as a part of the costs of the suit. The district courts are empowered, under the rules of the court governing actions at law, to make such order and enter such judgment, by writ of mandamus or otherwise, as may be appropriate to enforce or set aside the order of the division of the Adjustment Board: *Provided, however,* That such order may not be set aside except for failure of the division to comply with the requirements of this chapter, for failure of the order to conform, or confine itself, to matters within the scope of the division's jurisdiction, or for fraud or corruption by a member of the division making the order.

(q) If any employee or group of employees, or any carrier, is aggrieved by the failure of any division of the Adjustment Board to make an award in a dispute referred to it, or is aggrieved by any of the terms of an award or by the failure of the division to include certain terms in such award, then such employee or group of employees or carrier may file in any United States district court in which a petition under paragraph (p) could be filed, a petition for review of the division's order. A copy of the petition shall be forthwith transmitted by the clerk of the court to the Adjustment Board. The Adjustment Board shall file in the court the record of the proceedings on which it based its action. The court shall have jurisdiction to affirm the order of the division or to set it aside, in whole or in part, or it may remand the proceeding to the division for such further action as it may direct. On such review, the findings and order of the division shall be conclusive on the parties, except that the order of the division may be set aside, in whole or in part, or remanded to the division, for failure of the division to comply with the requirements of this chapter, for failure of the order to conform, or confine itself, to matters within the scope of the division's jurisdiction, or for fraud or corruption by a member of the division making the order. The judgment of the court shall be subject to review as provided in sections 1291 and 1254 of Title 28.

(r) All actions at law based upon the provisions of this section shall be begun within two years from the time the cause of action accrues under the award of the division of the Adjustment Board, and not after.

(s) The several divisions of the Adjustment Board shall maintain headquarters in Chicago, Illinois, meet regularly, and continue in session so long as there is pending before the division any matter within its jurisdiction which has been submitted for its consideration and which has not been disposed of.

(t) Whenever practicable, the several divisions or subdivisions of the Adjustment Board shall be supplied with suitable quarters in any Federal building located at its place of meeting.

(u) The Adjustment Board may, subject to the approval of the Mediation Board, employ and fix the compensations of such assistants as it deems necessary in carrying on its proceedings. The compensation of such employees shall be paid by the Mediation Board.

(v) The Adjustment Board shall meet within forty days after June 21, 1934, and adopt such rules as it deems necessary to control proceedings before the respective divisions and not in conflict with the provisions of this section. Immediately following the meeting of the entire Board and the adoption of such rules, the respective divisions shall meet and organize by the selection of a chairman, a vice chairman, and a secretary. Thereafter each division shall annually designate one of its members to act as chairman and one of its members to act as vice chairman: *Provided, however,* That the chairmanship and vice-chairmanship of any division shall alternate as between the groups, so that both the chairmanship and vice-chairmanship shall be held alternately by a representative of the carriers and a representative of the employees. In case of a vacancy, such vacancy shall be filled for the unexpired term by the selection of a successor from the same group.

(w) Each division of the Adjustment Board shall annually prepare and submit a report of its activities to the Mediation Board, and the substance of such report shall be included in the annual report of the Mediation Board to the Congress of the United States. The reports of each division of the Adjustment Board and the annual report of the Mediation Board shall state in detail all cases heard, all actions taken, the names, salaries, and duties of all agencies, employees, and officers receiving compensation from the United States under the authority of this chapter, and an account of all moneys appropriated by Congress pursuant to the authority conferred by this chapter and disbursed by such agencies, employees, and officers.

(x) Any division of the Adjustment Board shall have authority, in its discretion, to establish regional adjustment boards to act in its place and stead for such limited period as such division may determine to be necessary. Carrier members of such regional boards shall be designated in keeping with rules devised for this purpose by the carrier members of the Adjustment Board and the labor members shall be designated in keeping with rules devised for this purpose by the labor members of the Adjustment Board. Any such regional board shall, during the time for which it is appointed, have the same authority to conduct hearings, make findings upon disputes and adopt the same procedure as the division of the Adjustment Board appointing it, and its decisions shall be enforceable to the same extent and under the same processes. A neutral person, as referee, shall be appointed for service in connection with any such regional adjustment board in the same circumstances and manner as provided in paragraph (*l*) of this section, with respect to a division of the Adjustment Board.

Second. System, group, or regional boards: establishment by voluntary agreement; special adjustment boards: establishment, composition, designation of representatives by Mediation Board, neutral member, compensation, quorum, finality and enforcement of awards

Nothing in this section shall be construed to prevent any individual carrier, system, or group of carriers and any class or classes of its or their employees, all acting through their representatives, selected in accordance with the provisions of this chapter, from mutually agreeing to the establishment of system, group, or regional boards of adjustment for the purpose of adjusting and deciding disputes of the character specified in this section. In the event that either party to such a system, group, or regional board of adjustment is dissatisfied with such arrangement, it may upon ninety days' notice to the other party elect to come under the jurisdiction of the Adjustment Board.

If written request is made upon any individual carrier by the representative of any craft or class of employees of such carrier for the establishment of a special board of adjustment to resolve disputes otherwise referable to the Adjustment Board, or any dispute which has been pending before the Adjustment Board for twelve months from the date the dispute (claim) is received by the Board, or if any carrier makes such a request upon any such representative, the carrier or the representative upon whom such request is made shall join in an agreement establishing such a board within thirty days from the date such request is made. The cases which may be considered by such board shall be defined in the agreement establishing it. Such board shall consist of one person designated by the carrier and one person designated by the representative of the employees. If such carrier or such representative fails to agree upon the establishment of such a board as provided herein, or to exercise its rights to designate a member of the board, the carrier or representative making the request for the establishment of the special board may request the Mediation Board to designate a member of the special board on behalf of the carrier or representative upon whom such request was made. Upon receipt of a request for such designation the Mediation Board shall promptly make such designation and shall select an individual associated in interest with the carrier or representative he is to represent, who, with the member appointed by the carrier or representative requesting the establishment of the special board, shall constitute the board. Each member of the board shall be compensated by the party he is to represent. The members of the board so designated shall determine all matters not previously agreed upon by the carrier and the representa-

tive of the employees with respect to the establishment and jurisdiction
of the board. If they are unable to agree such matters shall be determined by a neutral member of the board selected or appointed and compensated in the same manner as is hereinafter provided with respect to
situations where the members of the board are unable to agree upon an
award. Such neutral member shall cease to be a member of the board
when he has determined such matters. If with respect to any dispute or
group of disputes the members of the board designated by the carrier
and the representative are unable to agree upon an award disposing of
the dispute or group of disputes they shall by mutual agreement select a
neutral person to be a member of the board for the consideration and
disposition of such dispute or group of disputes. In the event the members of the board designated by the parties are unable, within ten days
after their failure to agree upon an award, to agree upon the selection of
such neutral person, either member of the board may request the Mediation Board to appoint such neutral person and upon receipt of such request the Mediation Board shall promptly make such appointment. The
neutral person so selected or appointed shall be compensated and reimbursed for expenses by the Mediation Board. Any two members of the
board shall be competent to render an award. Such awards shall be final
and binding upon both parties to the dispute and if in favor of the petitioner, shall direct the other party to comply therewith on or before the
day named. Compliance with such awards shall be enforcible by proceedings in the United States district courts in the same manner and subject to the same provisions that apply to proceedings for enforcement of
compliance with awards of the Adjustment Board.

§4. (§154) National Mediation Board

**First. Board of Mediation abolished; National Mediation Board
established; composition; term of office; qualifications;
salaries; removal**

The Board of Mediation is abolished, effective thirty days from
June 21, 1934, and the members, secretary, officers, assistants, employees, and agents thereof, in office upon June 21, 1934, shall continue to
function and receive their salaries for a period of thirty days from such
date in the same manner as though this chapter had not been passed.
There is established, as an independent agency in the executive branch
of the Government, a board to be known as the "National Mediation
Board", to be composed of three members appointed by the President,

by and with the advice and consent of the Senate, not more than two of whom shall be of the same political party. Each member of the Mediation Board in office on January 1, 1965, shall be deemed to have been appointed for a term of office which shall expire on July I of the year his term would have otherwise expired. The terms of office of all successors shall expire three years after the expiration of the terms for which their predecessors were appointed; but any member appointed to fill a vacancy occurring prior to the expiration of the term for which his predecessor was appointed shall be appointed only for the unexpired term of his predecessor. Vacancies in the Board shall not impair the powers nor affect the duties of the Board nor of the remaining members of the Board. Two of the members in office shall constitute a quorum for the transaction of the business of the Board. Each member of the Board shall receive necessary traveling and subsistence expenses, or per them allowance in lieu thereof, subject to the provisions of law applicable thereto, while away from the principal office of the Board on business required by this chapter. No person in the employment of or who is pecuniarily or otherwise interested in any organization of emplorees or any carrier shall enter upon the duties of or continue to be a member of the Board. Upon the expiration of his term of office a member shall continue to serve until his successor is appointed and shall have qualified.

All cases referred to the Board of Mediation and unsettled on June 21, 1934, shall be handled to conclusion by the Mediation Board.

A member of the Board may be removed by the President for inefficiency, neglect of duty, malfeasance in office, or ineligibility, but for no other cause.

Second. Chairman; principal office; delegation of powers; oaths; seal; report

The Mediation Board shall annually designate a member to act as chairman. The Board shall maintain its principal office in the District of Columbia, but it may meet at any other place whenever it deems it necessary so to do. The Board may designate one or more of its members to exercise the functions of the Board in mediation proceedings. Each member of the Board shall have power to administer oaths and affirmations. The Board shall have a seal which shall be judicially noticed. The Board shall make an annual report to Congress.

Third. Appointment of experts and other employees; salaries of employees; expenditures

The Mediation Board may (1) subject to the provisions of the civil service laws, appoint such experts and assistants to act in a confidential capacity and such other officers and employees as are essential to the effective transaction of the work of the Board; (2) in accordance with chapter 51 and subchapter III of chapter 53 of Title 5, fix the salaries of such experts, assistants, officers, and employees; and (3) make such expenditures (including expenditures for rent and personal services at the seat of government and elsewhere, for law books, periodicals, and books of reference, and for printing and binding, and including expenditures for salaries and compensation, necessary traveling expenses and expenses actually incurred for subsistence, and other necessary expenses of the Mediation Board, Adjustment Board, Regional Adjustment Boards established under paragraph (w) of section 153 of this title, and boards of arbitration, in accordance with the provisions of this section and sections 153 and 157 of this title, respectively), as may be necessary for the execution of the functions vested in the Board, in the Adjustment Board and in the boards of arbitration, and as may be provided for by the Congress from time to time. All expenditures of the Board shall be allowed and paid on the presentation of itemized vouchers therefor approved by the chairman.

Fourth. Delegation of powers and duties

The Mediation Board is authorized by its order to assign, or refer, any portion of its work, business, or functions arising under this chapter or any other Act of Congress, or referred to it by Congress or either branch thereof, to an individual member of the Board or to an employee or employees of the Board to be designated by such order for action thereon, and by its order at any time to amend, modify, supplement, or rescind any such assignment or reference. All such orders shall take effect forthwith and remain in effect until otherwise ordered by the Board. In conformity with and subject to the order or orders of the Mediation Board in the premises, [and] such individual member of the Board or employee designated shall have power and authority to act as to any of said work, business, or functions so assigned or referred to him for action by the Board.

Fifth. Transfer of officers and employees of Board of Mediation; transfer of appropriation

All officers and employees of the Board of Mediation (except the members thereof, whose offices are abolished) whose services in the judgment of the Mediation Board are necessary to the efficient operation of the Board are transferred to the Board, without change in classification or compensation; except that the Board may provide for the adjustment of such classification or compensation to conform to the duties to which such officers and employees may be assigned.

All unexpended appropriations for the operation of the Board of Mediation that are available at the time of the abolition of the Board of Mediation shall be transferred to the Mediation Board and shall be available for its use for salaries and other authorized expenditures.

§5. (§155) Functions of Mediation Board

First. Disputes within jurisdiction of Mediation Board

The parties, or either party, to a dispute between an employee or group of employees and a carrier may invoke the services of the Mediation Board in any of the following cases:

(a) A dispute concerning changes in rates of pay, rules, or working conditions not adjusted by the parties in conference.

(b) Any other dispute not referable to the National Railroad Adjustment Board and not adjusted in conference between the parties or where conferences are refused.

The Mediation Board may proffer its services in case any labor emergency is found by it to exist at any time.

In either event the said Board shall promptly put itself in communication with the parties to such controversy, and shall use its best efforts, by mediation, to bring them to agreement. If such efforts to bring about an amicable settlement through mediation shall be unsuccessful, the said Board shall at once endeavor as its final required action (except as provided in paragraph third of this section and in section 160 of this title) to induce the parties to submit their controversy to arbitration, in accordance with the provisions of this chapter.

If arbitration at the request of the Board shall be refused by one or both parties, the Board shall at once notify both parties in writing that its mediatory efforts have failed and for thirty days thereafter, unless in the intervening period the parties agree to arbitration, or an emergency board shall be created under section 160 of this title, no change shall be made in the rates of pay, rules, or working conditions or established practices in effect prior to the time the dispute arose.

Second. Interpretation of agreement

In any case in which a controversy arises over the meaning or the application of any agreement reached through mediation under the provisions of this chapter, either party to the said agreement, or both, may apply to the Mediation Board for an interpretation of the meaning or application of such agreement. The said Board shall upon receipt of such request notify the parties to the controversy, and after a hearing of both sides give its interpretation within thirty days.

Third. Duties of Board with respect to arbitration of disputes; arbitrators; acknowledgment of agreement; notice to arbitrators; reconvening of arbitrators; filing contracts with Board; custody of records and documents

The Mediation Board shall have the following duties with respect to the arbitration of disputes under section 157 of this title:

(a) On failure of the arbitrators named by the parties to agree on the remaining arbitrator or arbitrators within the time set by section 157 of this title, it shall be the duty of the Mediation Board to name such remaining arbitrator or arbitrators. It shall be the duty of the Board in naming such arbitrator or arbitrators to appoint only those whom the Board shall deem wholly disinterested in the controversy to be arbitrated and impartial and without bias as between the parties to such arbitration. Should, however, the Board name an arbitrator or arbitrators not so disinterested and impartial, then, upon proper investigation and presentation of the facts, the Board shall promptly remove such arbitrator.

If an arbitrator named by the Mediation Board, in accordance with the provisions of this chapter, shall be removed by such Board as provided by this chapter, or if such an arbitrator refuses or is unable to serve, it shall be the duty of the Mediation Board, promptly, to select another arbitrator, in the same manner as provided in this chapter for an original appointment by the Mediation Board.

(b) Any member of the Mediation Board is authorized to take the acknowledgment of an agreement to arbitrate under this chapter. When so acknowledged, or when acknowledged by the parties before a notary public or the clerk of a district court or a court of appeals of the United

States, such agreement to arbitrate shall be delivered to a member of said Board or transmitted to said Board, to be filed in its office.

(c) When an agreement to arbitrate has been filed with the Mediation Board, or with one of its members, as provided by this section, and when the said Board has been furnished the names of the arbitrators chosen by the parties to the controversy it shall be the duty of the Board to cause a notice in writing to be served upon said arbitrators, notifying them of their appointment, requesting them to meet promptly to name the remaining arbitrator or arbitrators necessary to complete the Board of Arbitration, and advising them of the period within which, as provided by the agreement to arbitrate, they are empowered to name such arbitrator or arbitrators.

(d) Either party to an arbitration desiring the reconvening of a board of arbitration to pass upon any controversy arising over the meaning or application of an award may so notify the Mediation Board in writing, stating in such notice the question or questions to be submitted to such reconvened Board. The Mediation Board shall thereupon promptly communicate with the members of the Board of Arbitration, or a sub-committee of such Board appointed for such purpose pursuant to a provision in the agreement to arbitrate, and arrange for the reconvening of said Board of Arbitration or subcommittee, and shall notify the respective parties to the controversy of the time and place at which the Board, or the subcommittee, will meet for hearings upon the matters in controversy to be submitted to it. No evidence other than that contained in the record filed with the original award shall be received or considered by such reconvened Board or subcommittee, except such evidence as may be necessary to illustrate the interpretations suggested by the parties. If any member of the original Board is unable or unwilling to serve on such reconvened Board or subcommittee thereof, another arbitrator shall be named in the same manner and with the same powers and duties as such original arbitrator.

(e) Within sixty days after June 21, 1934, every carrier shall file with the Mediation Board a copy of each contract with its employees in effect on the 1st day of April 1934, covering rates of pay, rules, and working conditions. If no contract with any craft or class of its employees has been entered into, the carrier shall file with the Mediation Board a statement of that fact, including also a statement of the rates of pay, rules, and working conditions applicable in dealing with such craft or class. When any new contract is executed or change is made in an existing contract with any class or craft of its employees covering rates of pay, rules, or working conditions, or in those rates of pay, rules, and working conditions of employees not covered by contract, the carrier shall file the same with the Mediation Board within thirty days after such new contract or change in existing contract has been executed or rates of pay, rules, and working conditions have been made effective.

(f) The Mediation Board shall be the custodian of all papers and documents heretofore filed with or transferred to the Board of Mediation bearing upon the settlement, adjustment, or determination of disputes between carriers and their employees or upon mediation or arbitration proceedings held under or pursuant to the provisions of any Act of Congress in respect thereto; and the President is authorized to designate a custodian of the records and property of the Board of Mediation until the transfer and delivery of such records to the Mediation Board and to require the transfer and delivery to the Mediation Board of any and all such papers and documents filed with it or in its possession.

§6. (§156) Procedure in changing rates of pay, rules, and working conditions

Carriers and representatives of the employees shall give at least thirty days' written notice of an intended change in agreements affecting rates of pay, rules, or working conditions, and the time and place for the beginning of conference between the representatives of the parties interested in such intended changes shall be agreed upon within ten days after the receipt of said notice, and said time shall be within the thirty days provided in the notice. In every case where such notice of intended change has been given, or conferences are being held with reference thereto, or the services of the Mediation Board have been requested by either party, or said Board has proffered its services, rates of pay, rules, or working conditions shall not be altered by the carrier until the controversy has been finally acted upon, as required by section 155 of this title, by the Mediation Board, unless a period of ten days has elapsed after termination of conferences without request for or proffer of the services of the Mediation Board.

§7. (§157) Arbitration

First. Submission of controversy to arbitration

Whenever a controversy shall arise between a carrier or carriers and its or their employees which is not settled either in conference between representatives of the parties or by the appropriate adjustment board or through mediation, in the manner provided in sections 151 to 156 of this title, such controversy may, by agreement of the parties to such controversy, be submitted to the arbitration of a board of three (or, if the parties to the controversy so stipulate, of six) persons: *Provided, however,* That the failure or refusal of either party to submit a controversy to arbitration shall not be construed as a violation of any legal obligation imposed upon such party by the terms of this chapter or otherwise.

Second. Manner of selecting board of arbitration

Such board of arbitration shall be chosen in the following manner:

(a) In the case of a board of three the carrier or carriers and the representatives of the employees, parties respectively to the agreement to arbitrate, shall each name one arbitrator; the two arbitrators thus chosen shall select a third arbitrator. If the arbitrators chosen by the parties shall fail to name the third arbitrator within five days after their first meeting, such third arbitrator shall be named by the Mediation Board.

(b) In the case of a board of six the carrier or carriers and the representatives of the employees, parties respectively to the agreement to arbitrate, shall each name two arbitrators; the four arbitrators thus chosen shall, by a majority vote, select the remaining two arbitrators. If the arbitrators chosen by the parties shall fail to name the two arbitrators within fifteen days after their first meeting, the said two arbitrators, or as many of them as have not been named, shall be named by the Mediation Board.

Third. Board of arbitration; organization; compensation; procedure

(a) Notice of selection or failure to select arbitrators. When the arbitrators selected by the respective parties have agreed upon the remaining arbitrator or arbitrators, they shall notify the Mediation Board; and, in the event of their failure to agree upon any or upon all of the necessary arbitrators within the period fixed by this chapter, they shall, at the expiration of such period, notify the Mediation Board of the arbitrators selected, if any, or of their failure to make or to complete such selection.

(b) Organization of board; procedure. The board of arbitration shall organize and select its own chairman and make all necessary rules for conducting its hearings: *Provided, however,* That the board of arbitration shall be bound to give the parties to the controversy a full and fair hearing, which shall include an opportunity to present evidence in support of their claims, and an opportunity to present their case in per-

son, by counsel, or by other representative as they may respectively elect.

(c) Duty to reconvene; questions considered. Upon notice from the Mediation Board that the parties, or either party, to an arbitration desire the reconvening of the board of arbitration (or a subcommittee of such board of arbitration appointed for such purpose pursuant to the agreement to arbitrate) to pass upon any controversy over the meaning or application of their award, the board, or its subcommittee, shall at once reconvene. No question other than, or in addition to, the questions relating to the meaning or application of the award, submitted by the party or parties in writing, shall be considered by the reconvened board of arbitration or its subcommittee.

Such rulings shall be acknowledged by such board or subcommittee thereof in the same manner, and filed in the same district court clerk's office, as the original award and become a part thereof.

(d) Competency of arbitrators. No arbitrator, except those chosen by the Mediation Board, shall be incompetent to act as an arbitrator because of his interest in the controversy to be arbitrated, or because of his connection with or partiality to either of the parties to the arbitration.

(e) Compensation and expenses. Each member of any board of arbitration created under the provisions of this chapter named by either party to the arbitration shall be compensated by the party naming him. Each arbitrator selected by the arbitrators or named by the Mediation Board shall receive from the Mediation Board such compensation as the Mediation Board may fix, together with his necessary traveling expenses and expenses actually incurred for subsistence, while serving as an arbitrator.

(f) Award; disposition of original and copies. The board of arbitration shall furnish a certified copy of its award to the respective parties to the controversy, and shall transmit the original, together with the papers and proceedings and a transcript of the evidence taken at the hearings, certified under the hands of at least a majority of the arbitrators, to the clerk of the district court of the United States for the district wherein the controversy arose or the arbitration is entered into, to be filed in said clerk's office as hereinafter provided. The said board shall also furnish a certified copy of its award, and the papers and proceedings, including testimony relating thereto, to the Mediation Board to be filed in its office; and in addition a certified copy of its award shall be filed in the office of the Interstate Commerce Commission: *Provided, however,* That such award shall not be construed to diminish or extinguish any of the

powers or duties of the Interstate Commerce Commission, under subtitle IV of Title 49.*

(g) Compensation of assistants to board of arbitration; expenses; quarters. A board of arbitration may, subject to the approval of the Mediation Board, employ and fix the compensation of such assistants as it deems necessary in carrying on the arbitration proceedings. The compensation of such employees, together with their necessary traveling expenses and expenses actually incurred for subsistence, while so employed, and the necessary expenses of boards of arbitration, shall be paid by the Mediation Board.

Whenever practicable, the board shall be supplied with suitable quarters in any Federal building located at its place of meeting or at any place where the board may conduct its proceedings or deliberations.

(h) Testimony before board; oaths; attendance of witnesses; production of documents; subpoenas; fees. All testimony before said board shall be given under oath or affirmation, and any member of the board shall have the power to administer oaths or affirmations. The board of arbitration, or any member thereof, shall have the power to require the attendance of witnesses and the production of such books, papers, contracts, agreements, and documents as may be deemed by the board of arbitration material to a just determination of the matters submitted to its arbitration, and may for that purpose request the clerk of the district court of the United States for the district wherein said arbitration is being conducted to issue the necessary subpoenas, and upon such request the said clerk or his duly authorized deputy shall be, and he is, authorized, and it shall be his duty, to issue such subpoenas.

Any witness appearing before a board of arbitration shall receive the same fees and mileage as witnesses in courts of the United States, to be paid by the party securing the subpoena.

§8. (§158) Agreement to arbitrate; form and contents; signatures and acknowledgment; revocation

The agreement to arbitrate —

(a) Shall be in writing;

(b) Shall stipulate that the arbitration is held under the provisions of this chapter;

---

*The Interstate Commerce Commission was abolished, and its functions transferred to the Surface Transportation Board, effective Jan. 1, 1996. See Pub. L. 104-88, especially §205 (Dec. 29, 1995), 109 Stat. 803.

(c) Shall state whether the board of arbitration is to consist of three or of six members;

(d) Shall be signed by the duly accredited representatives of the carrier or carriers and the employees, parties respectively to the agreement to arbitrate, and shall be acknowledged by said parties before a notary public, the clerk of a district court or court of appeals of the United States, or before a member of the Mediation Board, and, when so acknowledged, shall be filed in the office of the Mediation Board;

(e) Shall state specifically the questions to be submitted to the said board for decision; and that, in its award or awards, the said board shall confine itself strictly to decisions as to the questions so specifically submitted to it;

(f) Shall provide that the questions, or any one or more of them, submitted by the parties to the board of arbitration may be withdrawn from arbitration on notice to that effect signed by the duly accredited representatives of all the parties and served on the board of arbitration;

(g) Shall stipulate that the signatures of a majority of said board of arbitration affixed to their award shall be competent to constitute a valid and binding award;

(h) Shall fix a period from the date of the appointment of the arbitrator or arbitrators necessary to complete the board (as provided for in the agreement) within which the said board shall commence its hearings;

(i) Shall fix a period from the beginning of the hearings within which the said board shall make and file its award: *Provided,* That the parties may agree at any time upon an extension of this period;

(j) Shall provide for the date from which the award shall become effective and shall fix the period during which the award shall continue in force;

(k) Shall provide that the award of the board of arbitration and the evidence of the proceedings before the board relating thereto, when certified under the hands of at least a majority of the arbitrators, shall be filed in the clerk's office of the district court of the United States for the district wherein the controversy arose or the arbitration was entered into, which district shall be designated in the agreement; and, when so filed, such award and proceedings shall constitute the full and complete record of the arbitration;

(*l*) Shall provide that the award, when so filed, shall be final and conclusive upon the parties as to the facts determined by said award and as to the merits of the controversy decided;

(m) Shall provide that any difference arising as to the meaning, or the application of the provisions, of an award made by a board of arbitration shall be referred back for a ruling to the same board, or, by agreement, to a subcommittee of such board; and that such ruling, when acknowledged in the same manner, and filed in the same district court clerk's office, as the original award, shall be a part of and shall have the same force and effect as such original award; and

(n) Shall provide that the respective parties to the award will each faithfully execute the same.

The said agreement to arbitrate, when properly signed and acknowledged as herein provided, shall not be revoked by a party to such agreement: *Provided, however,* That such agreement to arbitrate may at any time be revoked and canceled by the written agreement of both parties, signed by their duly accredited representatives, and (if no board of arbitration has yet been constituted under the agreement) delivered to the Mediation Board or any member thereof; or, if the board of arbitration has been constituted as provided by this chapter, delivered to such board of arbitration.

§9. (§159) Award and judgment thereon; effect of chapter on individual employee

First. Filing of award

The award of a board of arbitration, having been acknowledged as herein provided, shall be filed in the clerk's office of the district court designated in the agreement to arbitrate.

Second. Conclusiveness of award; judgment

An award acknowledged and filed as herein provided shall be conclusive on the parties as to the merits and facts of the controversy submitted to arbitration, and unless, within ten days after the filing of the award, a petition to impeach the award, on the grounds hereinafter set forth, shall be filed in the clerk's office of the court in which the award has been filed, the court shall enter judgment on the award, which judgment shall be final and conclusive on the parties.

Third. Impeachment of awards; grounds

Such petition for the impeachment or contesting of any award so filed shall be entertained by the court only on one or more of the following grounds:

(a) That the award plainly does not conform to the substantive requirements laid down by this chapter for such awards, or that the proceedings were not substantially in conformity with this chapter;

(b) That the award does not conform, nor confine itself, to the stipulations of the agreement to arbitrate; or

(c) That a member of the board of arbitration rendering the award was guilty of fraud or corruption; or that a party to the arbitration practiced fraud or corruption which fraud or corruption affected the result of the arbitration: *Provided, however,* That no court shall entertain any such petition on the ground that an award is invalid for uncertainty; in such case the proper remedy shall be a submission of such award to a reconvened board, or subcommittee thereof, for interpretation, as provided by this chapter: *Provided further,* That an award contested as herein provided shall be construed liberally by the court, with a view to favoring its validity, and that no award shall be set aside for trivial irregularity or clerical error, going only to form and not to substance.

Fourth. Effect of partial invalidity of award

If the court shall determine that a part of the award is invalid on some ground or grounds designated in this section as a ground of invalidity, but shall determine that a part of the award is valid, the court shall set aside the entire award: *Provided, however,* That, if the parties shall agree thereto, and if such valid and invalid parts are separable, the court shall set aside the invalid part, and order judgment to stand as to the valid part.

Fifth. Appeal; record

At the expiration of 10 days from the decision of the district court upon the petition filed as aforesaid, final judgment shall be entered in accordance with said decision, unless during said 10 days either party shall appeal therefrom to the court of appeals. In such case only such portion of the record shall be transmitted to the appellate court as is necessary to the proper understanding and consideration of the questions of law presented by said petition and to be decided.

Sixth. Finality of decision of court of appeals

The determination of said court of appeals upon said questions shall be final, and, being certified by the clerk thereof to said district court, judgment pursuant thereto shall thereupon be entered by said district court.

Seventh. Judgment where petitioner's contentions are sustained

If the petitioner's contentions are finally sustained, judgment shall be entered setting aside the award in whole or, if the parties so agree, in part; but in such case the parties may agree upon a judgment to be entered disposing of the subject matter of the controversy, which judgment when entered shall have the same force and effect as judgment entered upon an award.

Eighth. Duty of employee to render service without consent; right to quit

Nothing in this chapter shall be construed to require an individual employee to render labor or service without his consent, nor shall anything in this chapter be construed to make the quitting of his labor or service by an individual employee an illegal act; nor shall any court issue any process to compel the performance by an individual employee of such labor or service, without his consent.

§9A. (§159a) Special procedure for commuter service[*]

(a) Applicability of provisions. Except as provided in section 590(h) of this title, the provisions of this section shall apply to any dispute subject to this chapter between a publicly funded and publicly operated carrier providing rail commuter service (including the Amtrak Commuter Services Corporation) and its employees.

(b) Request for establishment of emergency board. If a dispute between the parties described in subsection (a) of this section is not adjusted under the foregoing provisions of this chapter and the President does not, under section 160 of this title, create an emergency board to investigate and report on such dispute, then any party to the dispute or the Governor of any State through which the service that is the subject of the dispute is operated may request the President to establish such an emergency board.

(c) Establishment of emergency board. (1) Upon the request of a party or a Governor under subsection (b) of this section, the President

---

[*]This section was added by Pub. L. 97-35, Title XI, §1157, 95 Stat. 681 (1981).

shall create an emergency board to investigate and report on the dispute in accordance with section 160 of this title. For purposes of this subsection, the period during which no change, except by agreement, shall be made by the parties in the conditions out of which the dispute arose shall be 120 days from the day of the creation of such emergency board.

(2) If the President, in his discretion, creates a board to investigate and report on a dispute between the parties described in subsection (a) of this section, the provisions of this section shall apply to the same extent as if such board had been created pursuant to paragraph (1) of this subsection.

(d) Public hearing by National Mediation Board upon failure of emergency board to effectuate settlement of dispute. Within 60 days after the creation of an emergency board under this section, if there has been no settlement between the parties, the National Mediation Board shall conduct a public hearing on the dispute at which each party shall appear and provide testimony setting forth the reasons it has not accepted the recommendations of the emergency board for settlement of the dispute.

(e) Establishment of second emergency board. If no settlement in the dispute is reached at the end of the 120-day period beginning on the date of the creation of the emergency board, any party to the dispute or the Governor of any State through which the service that is the subject of the dispute is operated may request the President to establish another emergency board, in which case the President shall establish such emergency board.

(f) Submission of final offers to second emergency board by parties. Within 30 days after creation of a board under subsection (e) of this section, the parties to the dispute shall submit to the board final offers for settlement of the dispute.

(g) Report of second emergency board. Within 30 days after the submission of final offers under subsection (f) of this section, the emergency board shall submit a report to the President setting forth its selection of the most reasonable offer.

(h) Maintenance of status quo during dispute period. From the time a request to establish a board is made under subsection (e) of this section until 60 days after such board makes its report under subsection (g) of this section, no change, except by agreement, shall be made by the parties in the conditions out of which the dispute arose.

(i) Work stoppages by employees subsequent to carrier offer selected; eligibility of employees for benefits. If the emergency board selects the final offer submitted by the carrier and, after the expiration of the 60-day period described in subsection (h) of this section, the em-

ployees of such carrier engage in any work stoppage arising out of the dispute, such employees shall not be eligible during the period of such work stoppage for benefits under the Railroad Unemployment Insurance Act [45 U.S.C. §351 et seq.].

(j) *Work stoppages by employees subsequent to employees offer selected; eligibility of employer for benefits.* If the emergency board selects the final offer submitted by the employees and, after the expiration of the 60-day period described in subsection (h) of this section, the carrier refuses to accept the final offer submitted by the employees and the employees of such carrier engage in any work stoppage arising out of the dispute, the carrier shall not participate in any benefits of any agreement between carriers which is designed to provide benefits to such carriers during a work stoppage.

§10. (§160) Emergency Board

If a dispute between a carrier and its employees be not adjusted under the foregoing provisions of this chapter and should, in the judgment of the Mediation Board, threaten substantially to interrupt interstate commerce to a degree such as to deprive any section of the country of essential transportation service, the Mediation Board shall notify the President, who may thereupon, in his discretion, create a board to investigate and report respecting such dispute. Such board shall be composed of such number of persons as to the President may seem desirable: *Provided, however,* That no member appointed shall be pecuniarily or otherwise interested in any organization of employees or any carrier. The compensation of the members of any such board shall be fixed by the President. Such board shall be created separately in each instance and it shall investigate promptly the facts as to the dispute and make a report thereon to the President within thirty days from the date of its creation.

There is authorized to be appropriated such sums as may be necessary for the expenses of such board, including the compensation and the necessary traveling expenses and expenses actually incurred for subsistence, of the members of the board. All expenditures of the board shall be allowed and paid on the presentation of itemized vouchers therefor approved by the chairman.

After the creation of such board and for thirty days after such board has made its report to the President, no change, except by agreement, shall be made by the parties to the controversy in the conditions out of which the dispute arose.

§11. (§161) Effect of partial invalidity of chapter

If any section, subsection, sentence, clause, or phrase of this chapter is for any reason held to be unconstitutional, such decision shall not affect the validity of the remaining portions of this chapter. All Acts or parts of Acts inconsistent with the provisions of this chapter are repealed.

§12. (§162) Authorization of appropriations

There is authorized to be appropriated such sums as may be necessary for expenditure by the Mediation Board in carrying out the provisions of this chapter.

§14. (§163) Repeal of prior legislation; exception

Chapters 6 and 7 of this title, providing for mediation, conciliation, and arbitration, and all Acts and parts of Acts in conflict with the provisions of this chapter are repealed, except that the members, secretary, officers, employees, and agents of the Railroad Labor Board, in office on May 20, 1926, shall receive their salaries for a period of 30 days from such date, in the same manner as though this chapter had not been passed.

SUBCHAPTER II.   CARRIERS BY AIR[*]

§201. (§181) Application of subchapter I to carriers by air

All of the provisions of subchapter I of this chapter except section 153 of this title are extended to and shall cover every common carrier by air engaged in interstate or foreign commerce, and every carrier by air transporting mail for or under contract with the United States Government, and every air pilot or other person who performs any work as an employee or subordinate official of such carrier or carriers, subject to its or their continuing authority to supervise and direct the manner of rendition of his service.

---

[*]Added April 10, 1936, c.166, 49 Stat. 1189 et seq.

§202. (§182) Duties, penalties, benefits, and privileges of subchapter I applicable

The duties, requirements, penalties, benefits, and privileges pre-scribed and established by the provisions of subchapter I of this chapter except section 153 of this title shall apply to said carriers by air and their employees in the same manner and to the same extent as though such carriers and their employees were specifically included within the definition of "carrier" and "employee", respectively, in section 151 of this title.

§203. (§183) Disputes within jurisdiction of Mediation Board

The parties or either party to a dispute between an employee or a group of employees and a carrier or carriers by air may invoke the ser-vices of the National Mediation Board and the jurisdiction of said Me-diation Board is extended to any of the following cases:

(a) A dispute concerning changes in rates of pay, rules, or work-ing conditions not adjusted by the parties in conference.

(b) Any other dispute not referable to an adjustment board, as hereinafter provided, and not adjusted in conference between the par-ties, or where conferences are refused.

The National Mediation Board may proffer its services in case any labor emergency is found by it to exist at any time.

The services of the Mediation Board may be invoked in a case un-der this subchapter in the same manner and to the same extent as are the disputes covered by section 155 of this title.

§204. (§184) System, group, or regional boards of adjustment

The disputes between an employee or group of employees and a carrier or carriers by air growing out of grievances, or out of the inter-pretation or application of agreements concerning rates of pay, rules, or working conditions, including cases pending and unadjusted on April 10, 1936 before the National Labor Relations Board, shall be handled in the usual manner up to and including the chief operating officer of the carrier designated to handle such disputes; but, failing to reach an ad-justment in this manner, the disputes may be referred by petition of the parties or by either party to an appropriate adjustment board, as hereinafter provided, with a full statement of the facts and supporting data bearing upon the disputes.

It shall be the duty of every carrier and of its employees, acting through their representatives, selected in accordance with the provisions of this subchapter, to establish a board of adjustment of jurisdiction not exceeding the jurisdiction which may be lawfully exercised by system, group, or regional boards of adjustment, under the authority of section 153 of this title.

Such boards of adjustment may be established by agreement between employees and carriers either on any individual carrier, or system, or group of carriers by air and any class or classes of its or their employees; or pending the establishment of a permanent National Board of Adjustment as hereinafter provided. Nothing in this chapter shall prevent said carriers by air, or any class or classes of their employees, both acting through their representatives selected in accordance with provisions of this subchapter, from mutually agreeing to the establishment of a National Board of Adjustment of temporary duration and of similarly limited jurisdiction.

§205. (§185) National Air Transport Adjustment Board

When, in the judgment of the National Mediation Board, it shall be necessary to have a permanent national board of adjustment in order to provide for the prompt and orderly settlement of disputes between said carriers by air, or any of them, and its or their employees, growing out of grievances or out of the interpretation or application of agreements between said carriers by air or any of them, and any class or classes of its or their employees, covering rates of pay, rules, or working conditions, the National Mediation Board is empowered and directed, by its order duly made, published, and served, to direct the said carriers by air and such labor organizations of their employees, national in scope, as have been or may be recognized in accordance with the provisions of this chapter, to select and designate four representatives who shall constitute a board which shall be known as the "National Air Transport Adjustment Board." Two members of said National Air Transport Adjustment Board shall be selected by said carriers by air and two members by the said labor organizations of the employees, within thirty days after the date of the order of the National Mediation Board, in the manner and by the procedure prescribed by section 153 of this title for the selection and designation of members of the National Railroad Adjustment Board. The National Air Transport Adjustment Board shall meet within forty days after the date of the order of the National Mediation Board directing the selection and designation of its members and shall organize and adopt rules for conducting its proceedings, in the manner prescribed in section 153 of this title. Vacancies in membership or office shall be filled, members shall be appointed in case of failure of the carriers or of labor organizations of the employees to select and designate representatives, members of the National Air Transport Adjustment Board shall be compensated, hearings shall be held, findings and awards made, stated, served, and enforced, and the number and compensation of any necessary assistants shall be determined and the compensation of such employees shall be paid, all in the same manner and to the same extent as provided with reference to the National Railroad Adjustment Board by section 153 of this title. The powers and duties prescribed and established by the provisions of section 153 of this title with reference to the National Railroad Adjustment Board and the several divisions thereof are conferred upon and shall be exercised and performed in like manner and to the same extent by the said National Air Transport Adjustment Board, not exceeding, however, the jurisdiction conferred upon said National Air Transport Adjustment Board by the provisions of this subchapter. From and after the organization of the National Air Transport Adjustment Board, if any system, group, or regional board of adjustment established by any carrier or carriers by air and any class or classes of its or their employees is not satisfactory to either party thereto, the said party, upon ninety days' notice to the other party, may elect to come under the jurisdiction of the National Air Transport Adjustment Board.

§207. (§187) Separability of provisions

If any provision of this subchapter or application thereof to any person or circumstance is held invalid, the remainder of such sections and the application of such provision to other persons or circumstances shall not be affected thereby.

§208. (§188) Authorization of appropriations

There is authorized to be appropriated such sums as may be necessary for expenditure by the Mediation Board in carrying out the provisions of this chapter.

Norris-LaGuardia Act of 1932
47 Stat. 70 (1932), as amended, 29 U.S.C. §§101-115

§1. (§101) Issuance of restraining orders and injunctions; limitation; public policy

No court of the United States, as defined in this chapter, shall have jurisdiction to issue any restraining order or temporary or permanent injunction in a case involving or growing out of a labor dispute, except in a strict conformity with the provisions of this chapter; nor shall any such restraining order or temporary or permanent injunction be issued contrary to the public policy declared in this chapter.

§2. (§102) Public policy in labor matters declared

In the interpretation of this chapter and in determining the jurisdiction and authority of the courts of the United States, as such jurisdiction and authority are defined and limited in this chapter, the public policy of the United States is declared as follows:

Whereas under prevailing economic conditions, developed with the aid of governmental authority for owners of property to organize in the corporate and other forms of ownership association, the individual unorganized worker is commonly helpless to exercise actual liberty of contract and to protect his freedom of labor, and thereby to obtain acceptable terms and conditions of employment, wherefore, though he should be free to decline to associate with his fellows, it is necessary that he have full freedom of association, self-organization, and designation of representatives of his own choosing, to negotiate the terms and conditions of his employment, and that he shall be free from the interference, restraint, or coercion of employers of labor, or their agents, in the designation of such representatives or in self-organization or in other concerted activities for the purpose of collective bargaining or other mutual aid or protection; therefore, the following definitions of and limitations upon the jurisdiction and authority of the courts of the United States are enacted.

§3. (§103) Nonenforceability of undertakings in conflict with public policy; "yellow dog" contracts

Any undertaking or promise, such as is described in this section, or any other undertaking or promise in conflict with the public policy declared in section 102 of this title, is declared to be contrary to the public policy of the United States, shall not be enforceable in any court of the United States and shall not afford any basis for the granting of legal or equitable relief by any such court, including specifically the following:

Every undertaking or promise hereafter made, whether written or oral, express or implied, constituting or contained in any contract or agreement of hiring or employment between any individual, firm, company, association, or corporation, and any employee or prospective employee of the same, whereby

(a) Either party to such contract or agreement undertakes or promises not to join, become, or remain a member of any labor organization or of any employer organization; or

(b) Either party to such contract or agreement undertakes or promises that he will withdraw from an employment relation in the event that he joins, becomes, or remains a member of any labor organization or of any employer organization.

§4. (§104) Enumeration of specific acts not subject to restraining orders or injunctions

No court of the United States shall have jurisdiction to issue any restraining order or temporary or permanent injunction in any case involving or growing out of any labor dispute to prohibit any person or persons participating or interested in such dispute (as these terms are herein defined) from doing, whether singly or in concert, any of the following acts:

(a) Ceasing or refusing to perform any work or to remain in any relation of employment;

(b) Becoming or remaining a member of any labor organization or of any employer organization, regardless of any such undertaking or promise as is described in section 103 of this title;

(c) Paying or giving to, or withholding from, any person participating or interested in such labor dispute, any strike or unemployment benefits or insurance, or other moneys or things of value;

(d) By all lawful means aiding any person participating or interested in any labor dispute who is being proceeded against in, or is prosecuting, any action or suit in any court of the United States or of any State;

(e) Giving publicity to the existence of, or the facts involved in, any labor dispute, whether by advertising, speaking, patrolling, or by any other method not involving fraud or violence;

(f) Assembling peaceably to act or to organize to act in promotion of their interests in a labor dispute;

(g) Advising or notifying any person of an intention to do any of the acts heretofore specified;

(h) Agreeing with other persons to do or not to do any of the acts heretofore specified; and

(i) Advising, urging, or otherwise causing or inducing without fraud or violence the acts heretofore specified, regardless of any such undertaking or promise as is described in section 103 of this title.

§5. (§105) Doing in concert of certain acts as constituting unlawful combination or conspiracy subjecting person to injunctive remedies

No court of the United States shall have jurisdiction to issue a restraining order or temporary or permanent injunction upon the ground that any of the persons participating or interested in a labor dispute constitute or are engaged in an unlawful combination or conspiracy because of the doing in concert of the acts enumerated in section 104 of this title.

§6. (§106) Responsibility of officers and members of associations or their organizations for unlawful acts of individual officers, members, and agents

No officer or member of any association or organization, and no association or organization participating or interested in a labor dispute, shall be held responsible or liable in any court of the United States for the unlawful acts of individual officers, members, or agents, except upon clear proof of actual participation in, or actual authorization of, such acts, or of ratification of such acts after actual knowledge thereof.

§7. (§107) Issuance of injunctions in labor disputes; hearing; findings of court; notice to affected persons; temporary restraining order; undertakings

No court of the United States shall have jurisdiction to issue a temporary or permanent injunction in any case involving or growing out of a labor dispute, as defined in this chapter, except after hearing the testimony of witnesses in open court (with opportunity for cross-examination) in support of the allegations of a complaint made under oath, and testimony in opposition thereto, if offered, and except after findings of fact by the court, to the effect —

   (a) That unlawful acts have been threatened and will be committed unless restrained or have been committed and will be continued unless restrained, but no injunction or temporary restraining order shall be issued on account of any threat or unlawful act excepting against the person or persons, association, or organization making the threat or committing the unlawful act or actually authorizing or ratifying the same after actual knowledge thereof;

   (b) That substantial and irreparable injury to complainant's property will follow;

   (c) That as to each item of relief granted greater injury will be inflicted upon complainant by the denial of relief than will be inflicted upon defendants by the granting of relief;

   (d) That complainant has no adequate remedy at law; and

   (e) That the public officers charged with the duty to protect complainant's property are unable or unwilling to furnish adequate protection.

Such hearing shall be held after due and personal notice thereof has been given, in such manner as the court shall direct, to all known persons against whom relief is sought, and also to the chief of those public officials of the county and city within which the unlawful acts have been threatened or committed charged with the duty to protect complainant's property: *Provided, however,* That if a complainant shall also allege that, unless a temporary restraining order shall be issued without notice, a substantial and irreparable injury to complainant's property will be unavoidable, such a temporary restraining order may be issued upon testimony under oath, sufficient, if sustained, to justify the court in issuing a temporary injunction upon a hearing after notice. Such a temporary restraining order shall be effective for no longer than five days and shall become void at the expiration of said five days. No temporary restraining order or temporary injunction shall be issued except on condition that complainant shall first file an undertaking with adequate security in an amount to be fixed by the court sufficient to recompense those enjoined for any loss, expense, or damage caused by the improvident or erroneous issuance of such order or injunction, including all reasonable costs (together with a reasonable attorney's fee) and expense of defense against the order or against the granting of any injunctive relief sought in the same proceeding and subsequently denied by the court.

The undertaking mentioned in this section shall be understood to signify an agreement entered into by the complainant and the surety upon which a decree may be rendered in the same suit or proceeding against said complainant and surety, upon a hearing to assess damages of which hearing complainant and surety shall have reasonable notice, the said complainant and surety submitting themselves to the jurisdiction of the court for that purpose. But nothing in this section contained shall deprive any party having a claim or cause of action under or upon such undertaking from electing to pursue his ordinary remedy by suit at law or in equity.

§8. (§108) Noncompliance with obligations involved in labor disputes or failure to settle by negotiation or arbitration as preventing injunctive relief

No restraining order or injunctive relief shall be granted to any complainant who has failed to comply with any obligation imposed by law which is involved in the labor dispute in question, or who has failed to make every reasonable effort to settle such dispute either by negotiation or with the aid of any available governmental machinery of mediation or voluntary arbitration.

§9. (§109) Granting of restraining order or injunction as dependent on previous findings of fact; limitation on prohibitions included in restraining orders and injunctions

No restraining order or temporary or permanent injunction shall be granted in a case involving or growing out of a labor dispute, except on the basis of findings of fact made and filed by the court in the record of the case prior to the issuance of such restraining order or injunction; and every restraining order or injunction granted in a case involving or growing out of a labor dispute shall include only a prohibition of such specific act or acts as may be expressly complained of in the bill of complaint or petition filed in such case and as shall be expressly included in said findings of fact made and filed by the court as provided in this chapter.

§10. (§110) Review by Court of Appeals of issuance or denial of temporary injunctions; record

Whenever any court of the United States shall issue or deny any temporary injunction in a case involving or growing out of a labor dispute, the court shall, upon the request of any party to the proceedings and on his filing the usual bond for costs, forthwith certify as in ordinary cases the record of the case to the court of appeals for its review. Upon the filing of such record in the court of appeals, the appeal shall be heard and the temporary injunctive order affirmed, modified, or set aside expeditiously.

§§11, 12. (§§111, 112) [Repealed June 25, 1948, c.645, §21, 62 Stat. 862, eff. Sept. 1, 1948.]

§13. (§113) Definitions of terms and words used in chapter

When used in this chapter, and for the purposes of this chapter —

(a) A case shall be held to involve or to grow out of a labor dispute when the case involves persons who are engaged in the same industry, trade, craft, or occupation; or have direct or indirect interests therein; or who are employees of the same employer; or who are members of the same or an affiliated organization of employers or employees; whether such dispute is (1) between one or more employers or associations of employers and one or more employees or associations of employees; (2) between one or more employers or associations of employers and one or more employers or associations of employers; or (3) between one or more employees or associations of employees and one or more employees or associations of employees; or when the case involves any conflicting or competing interests in a "labor dispute" (as defined in this section) of "persons participating or interested" therein (as defined in this section).

(b) A person or association shall be held to be a person participating or interested in a labor dispute if relief is sought against him or it, and if he or it is engaged in the same industry, trade, craft, or occupation in which such dispute occurs, or has a direct or indirect interest therein, or is a member, officer, or agent of any association composed in whole or in part of employers or employees engaged in such industry, trade, craft, or occupation.

(c) The term "labor dispute" includes any controversy concerning terms or conditions of employment, or concerning the association or representation of persons in negotiating, fixing, maintaining, changing, or seeking to arrange terms or conditions of employment, regardless of whether or not the disputants stand in the proximate relation of employer and employee.

(d) The term "court of the United States" means any court of the United States whose jurisdiction has been or may be conferred or defined or limited by Act of Congress, including the courts of the District of Columbia.

§14. (§114) Separability of provisions

If any provision of this chapter or the application thereof to any person or circumstance is held unconstitutional or otherwise invalid, the remaining provisions of this chapter and the application of such provisions to other persons or circumstances shall not be affected thereby.

§15. (§115) Repeal of conflicting acts

All acts and parts of acts in conflict with the provisions of this chapter are repealed.

National Labor Relations Act of 1935*
49 Stat. 449 (1935), as amended, 29 U.S.C. §§151-169

FINDINGS AND POLICIES

§1. (§151) The denial by **some** employers of the right of employees to organize and the refusal by **some** employers to accept the procedure of collective bargaining lead to strikes and other forms of industrial strife or unrest, which have the intent or the necessary effect of burdening or obstructing commerce by (a) impairing the efficiency, safety, or operation of the instrumentalities of commerce; (b) occurring in the current of commerce; (c) materially affecting, restraining, or controlling the flow of raw materials or manufactured or processed goods from or into the channels of commerce, or the prices of such materials or goods in commerce; or (d) causing diminution of employment and wages in such volume as substantially to impair or disrupt the market for goods flowing from or into the channels of commerce.

The inequality of bargaining power between employees who do not possess full freedom of association or actual liberty of contract, and employers who are organized in the corporate or other forms of ownership association substantially burdens and affects the flow of commerce, and tends to aggravate recurrent business depressions, by depressing wage rates and the purchasing power of wage earners in industry and by preventing the stabilization of competitive wage rates and working conditions within and between industries.

Experience has proved that protection by law of the right of employees to organize and bargain collectively safeguards commerce from injury, impairment, or interruption, and promotes the flow of commerce by removing certain recognized sources of industrial strife and unrest, by encouraging practices fundamental to the friendly adjustment of industrial disputes arising out of differences as to wages, hours, or other working conditions, and by restoring equality of bargaining power between employers and employees.

Experience has further demonstrated that certain practices by some labor organizations, their officers, and members have the in-

---

*Internal section references are to the NLRA of 1935 (Wagner Act), as amended, and not to the United States Code. The text of the original Wagner Act is printed in regular roman type; the Taft-Hartley amendments of 1947 are in boldface type; the Landrum-Griffin amendments of 1959 are in italics; and the 1974 amendments are underscored. Deleted matter is in brackets; bracketed matter in regular roman type was deleted in 1947; and bracketed matter in boldface type was deleted in 1959. Other amendments and deletions are specifically noted.—EDS.

tent or the necessary effect of burdening or obstructing commerce by preventing the free flow of goods in such commerce through strikes and other forms of industrial unrest or through concerted activities which impair the interest of the public in the free flow of such commerce. The elimination of such practices is a necessary condition to the assurance of the rights herein guaranteed.

It is hereby declared to be the policy of the United States to eliminate the causes of certain substantial obstructions to the free flow of commerce and to mitigate and eliminate these obstructions when they have occurred by encouraging the practice and procedure of collective bargaining and by protecting the exercise by workers of full freedom of association, self-organization, and designation of representatives of their own choosing, for the purpose of negotiating the terms and conditions of their employment or other mutual aid or protection.

DEFINITIONS

§2. (§152) When used in this Act —

(1) The term "person" includes one or more individuals, labor organizations, partnerships, associations, corporations, legal representatives, trustees, trustees in cases under Title 11,* or receivers.

(2) The term "employer" includes any person acting [in the interest of] **as an agent** of an employer, directly or indirectly, but shall not include the United States **or any wholly owned Government corporation, or any Federal Reserve Bank,** or any State or political subdivision thereof, [**or any corporation or association operating a hospital, if no part of the net earnings inures to the benefit of any private shareholder or individual,****] or any person subject to the Railway Labor Act, as amended from time to time, or any labor organization (other than when acting as an employer), or anyone acting in the capacity of officer or agent of such labor organization.

(3) The term "employee" shall include any employee, and shall not be limited to the employees of a particular employer, unless the Act explicitly states otherwise, and shall include any individual whose work has ceased as a consequence of, or in connection with, any current labor dispute or because of any unfair labor practice, and who has not obtained any other regular and substantially equivalent employment, but shall not include any individual employed as an agricultural laborer, or in the domestic service of any family or person at his home, or any indi-

---

*Bankruptcy. Provision as amended by Pub. L. 95-598, Nov. 6, 1978.
**The bracketed matter was deleted by Pub. L. 93-360, July 26, 1974.

vidual employed by his parent or spouse, **or any individual having the status of an independent contractor, or any individual employed as a supervisor, or any individual employed by an employer subject to the Railway Labor Act, as amended from time to time, or by any other person who is not an employer as herein defined.**

(4) The term "representatives" includes any individual or labor organization.

(5) The term "labor organization" means any organization of any kind, or any agency or employee representation committee or plan, in which employees participate and which exists for the purpose, in whole or in part, of dealing with employers concerning grievances, labor disputes, wages, rates of pay, hours of employment, or conditions of work.

(6) The term "commerce" means trade, traffic, commerce, transportation, or communication among the several States, or between the District of Columbia or any Territory of the United States and any State or other Territory, or between any foreign country and any State, Territory, or the District of Columbia, or within the District of Columbia or any Territory, or between points in the same State but through any other State or any Territory or the District of Columbia or any foreign country.

(7) The term "affecting commerce" means in commerce, or burdening or obstructing commerce or the free flow of commerce, or having led or tending to lead to a labor dispute burdening or obstructing commerce or the free flow of commerce.

(8) The term "unfair labor practice" means any unfair labor practice listed in section 8.

(9) The term "labor dispute" includes any controversy concerning terms, tenure or conditions of employment, or concerning the association or representation of persons in negotiating, fixing, maintaining, changing, or seeking to arrange terms or conditions of employment, regardless of whether the disputants stand in the proximate relation of employer and employee.

(10) The term "National Labor Relations Board" means the National Labor Relations Board provided for in section 3 of this Act.

(11) The term "supervisor" means any individual having authority, in the interest of the employer, to hire, transfer, suspend, lay off, recall, promote, discharge, assign, reward, or discipline other employees, or responsibly to direct them, or to adjust their grievances, or effectively to recommend such action, if in connection with the foregoing the exercise of such authority is not of a merely routine or clerical nature, but requires the use of independent judgment.

(12) The term "professional employee" means —

(a) any employee engaged in work (i) predominantly intellectual and varied in character as opposed to routine mental, manual, mechanical, or physical work; (ii) involving the consistent exercise of discretion and judgment in its performance; (iii) of such a character that the output produced or the result accomplished cannot be standardized in relation to a given period of time; (iv) requiring knowledge of an advanced type in a field of science or learning customarily acquired by a prolonged course of specialized intellectual instruction and study in an institution of higher learning or a hospital, as distinguished from a general academic education or from an apprenticeship or from training in the performance of routine mental, manual, or physical processes; or

(b) any employee, who (i) has completed the courses of specialized intellectual instruction and study described in clause (iv) of paragraph (a), and (ii) is performing related work under the supervision of a professional person to qualify himself to become a professional employee as defined in paragraph (a).

(13) In determining whether any person is acting as an "agent" of another person so as to make such other person responsible for his acts, the question of whether the specific acts performed were actually authorized or subsequently ratified shall not be controlling.

(14) The term "health care institution" shall include any hospital, convalescent hospital, health maintenance organization, health clinic, nursing home, extended care facility, or other institution devoted to the care of sick, infirm, or aged person (sic).

NATIONAL LABOR RELATIONS BOARD[*]

§3. (§153) (a) The National Labor Relations Board (hereinafter called the "Board") created by this Act prior to its amendment by the Labor Management Relations Act, 1947, is hereby continued as an agency of the United States, except that the Board shall consist of five instead of three members, appointed by the President by and with the advice and consent of the Senate. Of the two additional members so provided for, one shall be appointed for a term of five years and the other for a term of two years. Their successors, and

---

[*]Because §§3 and 4 were amended so extensively in 1947, the 1935 version of those sections is not reproduced below; only the 1947 and 1959 amendments are set forth.—EDS.

the successors of the other members, shall be appointed for terms of five years each, excepting that any individual chosen to fill a vacancy shall be appointed only for the unexpired term of the member whom he shall succeed. The President shall designate one member to serve as Chairman of the Board. Any member of the Board may be removed by the President, upon notice and hearing, for neglect of duty or malfeasance in office, but for no other cause.

(b) The Board is authorized to delegate to any group of three or more members any or all of the powers which it may itself exercise. *The Board is also authorized to delegate to its regional directors its powers under section 9 to determine the unit appropriate for the purpose of collective bargaining, to investigate and provide for hearings, and determine whether a question of representation exists, and to direct an election or take a secret ballot under subsection (c) or (e) of section 9 and certify the results thereof, except that upon the filing of a request therefor with the Board by any interested person, the Board may review any action of a regional director delegated to him under this paragraph, but such a review shall not, unless specifically ordered by the Board, operate as a stay of any action taken by the regional director.* A vacancy in the Board shall not impair the right of the remaining members to exercise all of the powers of the Board, and three members of the Board shall, at all times, constitute a quorum of the Board, except that two members shall constitute a quorum of any group designated pursuant to the first sentence hereof. The Board shall have an official seal which shall be judicially noticed.

(c) The Board shall at the close of each fiscal year make a report in writing to Congress and to the President summarizing significant case activities and operations for that fiscal year.[*]

(d) There shall be a General Counsel of the Board who shall be appointed by the President, by and with the advice and consent of the Senate, for a term of four years. The General Counsel of the Board shall exercise general supervision over all attorneys employed by the Board (other than administrative law judges[**] and legal assistants to Board members) and over the officers and employees in the regional offices. He shall have final authority, on behalf of the Board, in respect of the investigation of charges and issuance of complaints under section 10, and in respect of the prosecution of

---

[*]As amended by Pub. L. 93-608, Jan. 2, 1975, and Pub. L. 97-375, Dec. 21, 1982.

[**]"Administrative law judge" was substituted for "trial examiner" throughout the Act pursuant to §3105 of Title 5 and §3 of Pub. L. 95-251, Mar. 27, 1978, 92 Stat. 184.

such complaints before the Board, and shall have such other duties as the Board may prescribe or as may be provided by law. *In case of a vacancy in the office of the General Counsel the President is authorized to designate the officer or employee who shall act as General Counsel during such vacancy, but no person or persons so designated shall so act (1) for more than forty days when the Congress is in session unless a nomination to fill such vacancy shall have been submitted to the Senate, or (2) after the adjournment sine die of the session of the Senate in which such nomination was submitted.*

§4. (§154) (a) Each member of the Board and the General Counsel of the Board [shall receive a salary of $12,000 a year,[*]] shall be eligible for reappointment, and shall not engage in any other business, vocation, or employment. The Board shall appoint an executive secretary, and such attorneys, examiners, and regional directors, and such other employees as it may from time to time find necessary for the proper performance of its duties. The Board may not employ any attorneys for the purpose of reviewing transcripts of hearings or preparing drafts of opinions except that any attorney employed for assignment as a legal assistant to any Board member may for such Board member review such transcripts and prepare such drafts. No administrative law judge's report shall be reviewed, either before or after its publication, by any person other than a member of the Board or his legal assistant, and no administrative law judge shall advise or consult with the Board with respect to exceptions taken to his findings, rulings, or recommendations. The Board may establish or utilize such regional, local, or other agencies, and utilize such voluntary and uncompensated services, as may from time to time be needed. Attorneys appointed under this section may, at the direction of the Board, appear for and represent the Board in any case in court. Nothing in this Act shall be construed to authorize the Board to appoint individuals for the purpose of conciliation or mediation, or for economic analysis.

(b) All of the expenses of the Board, including all necessary traveling and subsistence expenses outside the District of Columbia incurred by the members or employees of the Board under its orders, shall be allowed and paid on the presentation of itemized vouchers therefor approved by the Board or by any individual it designates for that purpose.

---

[*]Deleted pursuant to §§5311 et seq. of Title V, Government Organization and Employees.

§5. (§155) The principal office of the Board shall be in the District of Columbia, but it may meet and exercise any or all of its powers at any other place. The Board may, by one or more of its members or by such agents or agencies as it may designate, prosecute any inquiry necessary to its functions in any part of the United States. A member who participates in such an inquiry shall not be disqualified from subsequently participating in a decision of the Board in the same case.

§6. (§156) The Board shall have authority from time to time to make, amend, and rescind, **in the manner prescribed by the Administrative Procedure Act,**[*] such rules and regulations as may be necessary to carry out the provisions of this Act. [Such rules and regulations shall be effective upon publication in the manner which the Board shall prescribe.]

RIGHTS OF EMPLOYEES

§7. (§157) Employees shall have the right to self-organization, to form, join, or assist labor organizations, to bargain collectively through representatives of their own choosing, and to engage in other concerted activities for the purpose of collective bargaining or other mutual aid or protection, **and shall also have the right to refrain from any or all of such activities except to the extent that such right may be affected by an agreement requiring membership in a labor organization as a condition of employment as authorized in section 8(a)(3).**

UNFAIR LABOR PRACTICES

§8. (§158) (a) It shall be an unfair labor practice for an employer —
   (1) to interfere with, restrain, or coerce employees in the exercise of the rights guaranteed in section 7;
   (2) to dominate or interfere with the formation or administration of any labor organization or contribute financial or other support to it: *Provided,* That subject to rules and regulations made and published by the Board pursuant to section 6, an employer shall not be prohibited from permitting employees to confer with him during working hours without loss of time or pay;

---

[*]5 U.S.C. §§551 et seq.—EDS.

(3) by discrimination in regard to hire or tenure of employment or any term or condition of employment to encourage or discourage membership in any labor organization: *Provided,* That nothing in this Act, or in any other statute of the United States, shall preclude an employer from making an agreement with a labor organization (not established, maintained, or assisted by any action defined in **section 8(a) of** this Act as an unfair labor practice) to require as a condition of employment membership therein **on or after the thirtieth day following the beginning of such employment or the effective date of such agreement, whichever is the later, (i)** if such labor organization is the representative of the employees as provided in section 9(a), in the appropriate collective-bargaining unit covered by such agreement when made, **[and has at the time the agreement was made or within the preceding twelve months received from the Board a notice of compliance with sections 9(f), (g), (h)], and (ii) unless following an election held as provided in section 9(e) within one year preceding the effective date of such agreement, the Board shall have certified that at least a majority of the employees eligible to vote in such election have voted to rescind the authority of such labor organization to make such an agreement:*** ***Provided further,* That no employer shall justify any discrimination against an employee for nonmembership in a labor organization (A) if he has reasonable grounds for believing that such membership was not available to the employee on the same terms and conditions generally applicable to other members, or (B) if he has reasonable grounds for believing that membership was denied or terminated for reasons other than the failure of the employee to tender the periodic dues and the initiation fees uniformly required as a condition of acquiring or retaining membership;**

(4) to discharge or otherwise discriminate against an employee because he has filed charges or given testimony under this Act;

(5) to refuse to bargain collectively with the representatives of his employees, subject to the provisions of section 9(a).

(b) It shall be an unfair labor practice for a labor organization or its agents —

(1) to restrain or coerce (A) employees in the exercise of the rights guaranteed in section 7: *Provided,* That this paragraph shall not impair the right of a labor organization to prescribe its own rules with respect to the acquisition or retention of membership therein; or (B) an employer in the selection of his represen-

---

*Clause (ii) was added in 1951 by 65 Stat. 601.

tatives for the purposes of collective bargaining or the adjustment of grievances;

(2) to cause or attempt to cause an employer to discriminate against an employee in violation of subsection (a)(3) or to discriminate against an employee with respect to whom membership in such organization has been denied or terminated on some ground other than his failure to tender the periodic dues and the initiation fees uniformly required as a condition of acquiring or retaining membership;

(3) to refuse to bargain collectively with an employer, provided it is the representative of his employees subject to the provisions of section 9(a);

(4)(*i*) to engage in, or to induce or encourage [the employees of any employer] *any individual employed by any person engaged in commerce or in an industry affecting commerce* to engage in, a strike or a [concerted] refusal in the course of [their] *his* employment to use, manufacture, process, transport, or otherwise handle or work on any goods, articles, materials, or commodities or to perform any services[,]*; or (ii) to threaten, coerce, or restrain any person engaged in commerce or in an industry affecting commerce,* where *in either case* an object thereof is —

(A) forcing or requiring any employer or self-employed person to join any labor or employer organization or [any employer or other person to cease using, selling, handling, transporting, or otherwise dealing in the products of any other producer, processor, or manufacturer, or to cease doing business with any other person] *to enter into any agreement which is prohibited by section (e);*

(B) *forcing or requiring any person to cease using, selling, handling, transporting, or otherwise dealing in the products of any other producer, processor, or manufacturer, or to cease doing business with any other person, or* forcing or requiring any other employer to recognize or bargain with a labor organization as the representative of his employees unless such labor organization has been certified as the representative of such employees under the provisions of section 9[;]*: Provided, That nothing contained in this clause (B) shall be construed to make unlawful, where not otherwise unlawful, any primary strike or primary picketing;*

(C) forcing or requiring any employer to recognize or bargain with a particular labor organization as the representative of his employees if another labor organization has been certified as the representative of such employees under the provisions of section 9;

(D) forcing or requiring any employer to assign particular work to employees in a particular labor organization or in a particular trade, craft, or class rather than to employees in another labor organization or in another trade, craft, or class, unless such employer is failing to conform to an order or certification of the Board determining the bargaining representative for employees performing such work:

Provided, That nothing contained in subsection (b) shall be construed to make unlawful a refusal by any person to enter upon the premises of any employer (other than his own employer), if the employees of such employer are engaged in a strike ratified or approved by a representative of such employees whom such employer is required to recognize under this Act[;]: *Provided further, That for the purposes of this paragraph (4) only, nothing contained in such paragraph shall be construed to prohibit publicity, other than picketing, for the purpose of truthfully advising the public, including consumers and members of a labor organization, that a product or products are produced by an employer with whom the labor organization has a primary dispute and are distributed by another employer, as long as such publicity does not have an effect of inducing any individual employed by any person other than the primary employer in the course of his employment to refuse to pick up, deliver, or transport any goods, or not to perform any services, at the establishment of the employer engaged in such distribution;*

(5) to require of employees covered by an agreement authorized under subsection (a)(3) of this section the payment, as a condition precedent to becoming a member of such organization, of a fee in an amount which the Board finds excessive or discriminatory under all the circumstances. In making such a finding, the Board shall consider, among other relevant factors, the practices and customs of labor organizations in the particular industry, and the wages currently paid to the employees affected; [and]

(6) to cause or attempt to cause an employer to pay or deliver or agree to pay or deliver any money or other thing of value, in the nature of an exaction, for services which are not performed or not to be performed[.]; *and*

(7) to picket or cause to be picketed, or threaten to picket or cause to be picketed, any employer where an object thereof is forcing or requiring an employer to recognize or bargain with a labor organization as the representative of his employees, or forcing or re-

quiring the employees of an employer to accept or select such labor organization as their collective bargaining representative, unless such labor organization is currently certified as the representative of such employees:

(A) where the employer has lawfully recognized in accordance with this Act any other labor organization and a question concerning representation may not appropriately be raised under section 9(c) of this Act,

(B) where within the preceding twelve months a valid election under section 9(c) of this Act has been conducted, or

(C) where such picketing has been conducted without a petition under section 9(c) of this Act being filed within a reasonable period of time not to exceed thirty days from the commencement of such picketing: Provided, That when such a petition has been filed the Board shall forthwith, without regard to the provisions of section 9(c)(1) of this Act or the absence of a showing of a substantial interest on the part of the labor organization, direct an election in such unit as the Board finds to be appropriate and shall certify the results thereof: Provided further, That nothing in this subparagraph (C) shall be construed to prohibit any picketing or other publicity for the purpose of truthfully advising the public (including consumers) that an employer does not employ members of, or have a contract with, a labor organization, unless an effect of such picketing is to induce any individual employed by any other person in the course of his employment, not to pick up, deliver or transport any goods or not to perform any services.

Nothing in this paragraph (7) shall be construed to permit any act which would otherwise be an unfair labor practice under this section 8(b).

(c) The expressing of any views, argument, or opinion, or the dissemination thereof, whether in written, printed, graphic, or visual form, shall not constitute or be evidence of an unfair labor practice under any of the provisions of this Act, if such expression contains no threat of reprisal or force or promise of benefit.

(d) For the purposes of this section, to bargain collectively is the performance of the mutual obligation of the employer and the representative of the employees to meet at reasonable times and confer in good faith with respect to wages, hours, and other terms and conditions of employment, or the negotiation of an agreement, or any question arising thereunder, and the execution of a written contract incorporating any agreement reached if requested by either party, but such obligation does not compel either party to agree to a proposal or require the making of a concession: *Provided,* That where there is in effect a collective-bargaining contract covering employees in an industry affecting commerce, the duty to bargain collectively shall also mean that no party to such contract shall terminate or modify such contract, unless the party desiring such termination or modification —

(1) serves a written notice upon the other party to the contract of the proposed termination or modification sixty days prior to the expiration date thereof, or in the event such contract contains no expiration date, sixty days prior to the time it is proposed to make such termination or modification;

(2) offers to meet and confer with the other party for the purpose of negotiating a new contract or a contract containing the proposed modifications;

(3) notifies the Federal Mediation and Conciliation Service within thirty days after such notice of the existence of a dispute, and simultaneously therewith notifies any State or Territorial agency established to mediate and conciliate disputes within the State or Territory where the dispute occurred, provided no agreement has been reached by that time; and

(4) continues in full force and effect, without resorting to strike or lock-out, all the terms and conditions of the existing contract for a period of sixty days after such notice is given or until the expiration date of such contract, whichever occurs later: The duties imposed upon employers, employees, and labor organizations by paragraphs (2), (3), and (4) shall become inapplicable upon an intervening certification of the Board, under which the labor organization or individual, which is a party to the contract, has been superseded as or ceased to be the representative of the employees subject to the provisions of section 9(a), and the duties so imposed shall not be construed as requiring either party to discuss or agree to any modification of the terms and conditions contained in a contract for a fixed period, if such modification is to become effective before such terms and conditions can be reopened under the provisions of the contract. Any employee who engages in a strike within the [sixty-day] any notice period specified in this subsection, or who engages in any strike within the appropriate period specified in subsection (g) of this section, shall lose his status as an employee of the employer engaged in the particular labor dispute, for the purposes of sections 8, 9, and 10 of this Act, but such loss of status for such employee shall terminate if and when he is reemployed by such employer. Whenever the collective bargaining involves employees of a

health care institution, the provisions of this subsection shall be modified as follows:

(A) The notice of paragraph (1) of this subsection shall be ninety days; the notice of paragraph (3) of this subsection shall be sixty days; and the contract period of paragraph (4) of this subsection shall be ninety days.

(B) Where the bargaining is for an initial agreement following certification or recognition, at least thirty days' notice of the existence of a dispute shall be given by the labor organization to the agencies set forth in paragraph (3) of this subsection.

(C) After notice is given to the Federal Mediation and Conciliation Service under either clause (A) or (B) of this sentence, the Service shall promptly communicate with the parties and use its best efforts, by mediation and conciliation, to bring them to agreement. The parties shall participate fully and promptly in such meetings as may be undertaken by the Service for the purpose of aiding in a settlement of the dispute.

(e) It shall be an unfair labor practice for any labor organization and any employer to enter into any contract or agreement, express or implied, whereby such employer ceases or refrains or agrees to cease or refrain from handling, using, selling, transporting or otherwise dealing in any of the products of any other employer, or to cease doing business with any other person, and any contract or agreement entered into heretofore or hereafter containing such an agreement shall be to such extent unenforcible (sic) *and void: Provided, That nothing in this subsection (e) shall apply to an agreement between a labor organization and an employer in the construction industry relating to the contracting or subcontracting of work to be done at the site of the construction, alteration, painting, or repair of a building, structure, or other work: Provided further, That for the purposes of this subsection (e) and subsection (b)(4)(B) of this section the terms "any employer", "any person engaged in commerce or an industry affecting commerce", and "any person" when used in relation to the terms "any other producer, processor, or manufacturer", "any other employer", or "any other person" shall not include persons in the relation of a jobber, manufacturer, contractor, or subcontractor working on the goods or premises of the jobber or manufacturer or performing parts of an integrated process of production in the apparel and clothing industry: Provided further, That nothing in this Act shall prohibit the enforcement of any agreement which is within the foregoing exception.*

(f) It shall not be an unfair labor practice under subsections (a) and (b) of this section for an employer engaged primarily in the building

*and construction industry to make an agreement covering employees engaged (or who, upon their employment, will be engaged) in the building and construction industry with a labor organization of which building and construction employees are members (not established, maintained, or assisted by any action defined in subsection (a) of this section as an unfair labor practice) because (1) the majority status of such labor organization has not been established under the provisions of section 9 of this Act prior to the making of such agreement, or (2) such agreement requires as a condition of employment, membership in such labor organization after the seventh day following the beginning of such employment or the effective date of the agreement, whichever is later, or (3) such agreement requires the employer to notify such labor organization of opportunities for employment with such employer, or gives such labor organization an opportunity to refer qualified applicants for such employment, or (4) such agreement specifies minimum training or experience qualifications for employment or provides for priority in opportunities for employment based upon length of service with such employer, in the industry or in the particular geographical area: Provided, That nothing in this subsection shall set aside the final proviso to section 8(a)(3) of this Act: Provided further, That any agreement which would be invalid, but for clause (1) of this subsection, shall not be a bar to a petition filed pursuant to section 9(c) or 9(e).**

(g) A labor organization before engaging in any strike, picketing, or other concerted refusal to work at any health care institution shall, not less than ten days prior to such action, notify the institution in writing and the Federal Mediation and Conciliation Service of that intention, except that in the case of bargaining for an initial agreement following certification or recognition the notice required by this subsection shall not be given until the expiration of the period specified in clause (B) of the last sentence of section (8)(d) of this Act. The notice shall state the date and time that such action will commence. The notice, once given, may be extended by the written agreement of both parties.

---

*Section 8(f) was inserted in the Act by §705(a) of Pub. L. 86-257, Sept. 14, 1959. Section 705(b) of that law provides:

Nothing contained in the amendment made by subsection (a) shall be construed as authorizing the execution or application of agreements requiring membership in a labor organization as a condition of employment in any State or Territory in which such execution or application is prohibited by State or Territorial Law.

REPRESENTATIVES AND ELECTIONS

§9. (§159) (a) Representatives designated or selected for the purposes of collective bargaining by the majority of the employees in a unit appropriate for such purposes, shall be the exclusive representatives of all the employees in such unit for the purposes of collective bargaining in respect to rates of pay, wages, hours of employment, or other conditions of employment: *Provided,* That any individual employee or a group of employees shall have the right at any time to present grievances to their employer **and to have such grievances adjusted, without the intervention of the bargaining representative, as long as the adjustment is not inconsistent with the terms of a collective-bargaining contract or agreement then in effect:** *Provided further,* **That the bargaining representative has been given opportunity to be present at such adjustment.**

(b) The Board shall decide in each case whether, in order to assure to employees the fullest freedom in exercising the rights guaranteed by this Act, the unit appropriate for the purposes of collective bargaining shall be the employer unit, craft unit, plant unit, or subdivision thereof: *Provided,* **That the Board shall not (1) decide that any unit is appropriate for such purposes if such unit includes both professional employees and employees who are not professional employees unless a majority of such professional employees vote for inclusion in such unit; or (2) decide that any craft unit is inappropriate for such purposes on the ground that a different unit has been established by a prior Board determination, unless a majority of the employees in the proposed craft unit vote against separate representation or (3) decide that any unit is appropriate for such purposes if it includes, together with other employees, any individual employed as a guard to enforce against employees and other persons rules to protect property of the employer or to protect the safety of persons on the employer's premises; but no labor organization shall be certified as the representative of employees in a bargaining unit of guards if such organization admits to membership, or is affiliated directly or indirectly with an organization which admits to membership, employees other than guards.**

[(c) Whenever a question affecting commerce arises concerning the representation of employees, the Board may investigate such controversy and certify to the parties, in writing, the name or names of the representatives that have been designated or selected. In any such investigation, the Board shall provide for an appropriate hearing upon due notice, either in conjunction with a proceeding under section 10 or otherwise, and may take a secret ballot of employees, or utilize any other suitable method to ascertain such representatives.]

(c)(1) Whenever a petition shall have been filed, in accordance with such regulations as may be prescribed by the Board—

(A) by an employee or group of employees or any individual or labor organization acting in their behalf alleging that a substantial number of employees (i) wish to be represented for collective bargaining and that their employer declines to recognize their representative as the representative defined in section 9(a), or (ii) assert that the individual or labor organization, which has been certified or is being currently recognized by their employer as the bargaining representative, is no longer a representative as defined in section 9(a); or

(B) by an employer, alleging that one or more individuals or labor organizations have presented to him a claim to be recognized as the representative defined in section 9(a);
the Board shall investigate such petition and if it has reasonable cause to believe that a question of representation affecting commerce exists shall provide for an appropriate hearing upon due notice. Such hearing may be conducted by an officer or employee of the regional office, who shall not make any recommendations with respect thereto. If the Board finds upon the record of such hearing that such a question of representation exists, it shall direct an election by secret ballot and shall certify the results thereof.

(2) In determining whether or not a question of representation affecting commerce exists, the same regulations and rules of decision shall apply irrespective of the identity of the persons filing the petition or the kind of relief sought and in no case shall the Board deny a labor organization a place on the ballot by reason of an order with respect to such labor organization or its predecessor not issued in conformity with section 10(c).

(3) No election shall be directed in any bargaining unit or any subdivision within which in the preceding twelve-month period, a valid election shall have been held. Employees [on strike] *engaged in an economic strike* who are not entitled to reinstatement shall [not] be eligible to vote *under such regulations as the Board shall find are consistent with the purposes and provisions of this Act in any election conducted within twelve months after the commencement of the strike.* In any election where none of the choices on the ballot receives a majority, a run-off shall be conducted, the ballot providing for a selection between the two choices receiving the

largest and second largest number of valid votes cast in the election.

(4) Nothing in this section shall be construed to prohibit the waiving of hearings by stipulation for the purpose of a consent election in conformity with regulations and rules of decision of the Board.

(5) In determining whether a unit is appropriate for the purposes specified in subsection (b) of this section the extent to which the employees have organized shall not be controlling.

(d) Whenever an order of the Board made pursuant to section 10(c) is based in whole or in part upon facts certified following an investigation pursuant to subsection (c) of this section and there is a petition for the enforcement or review of such order, such certification and the record of such investigation shall be included in the transcript of the entire record required to be filed under section 10(e) or 10(f), and thereupon the decree of the court enforcing, modifying, or setting aside in whole or in part the order of the Board shall be made and entered upon the pleadings, testimony, and proceedings set forth in such transcript.

(e)(1) Upon the filing with the Board, by 30 per centum or more of the employees in a bargaining unit covered by an agreement between their employer and a labor organization made pursuant to section 8(a)(3), of a petition alleging they desire that such authority be rescinded, the Board shall take a secret ballot of the employees in such unit and shall certify the results thereof to such labor organization and to the employer.

(2) No election shall be conducted pursuant to this subsection in any bargaining unit or any subdivision within which, in the preceding twelve-month period, a valid election shall have been held.[*]

[Subsections (f), (g), and (h) were deleted by the Labor-Management Reporting and Disclosure Act of 1959. — EDS.]

---

[*]As enacted in 1947, Section 9(e) had three subsections. In 1951, the first subsection was deleted, and the two remaining subsections were renumbered (1) and (2). 65 Stat. 601. The deleted subsection required, as a prerequisite to the inclusion of a union security clause in a labor agreement, authorization by a majority of unit employees in a Board-conducted election.—EDS.

Prevention of Unfair Labor Practices

§10. (§160) (a) The Board is empowered, as hereinafter provided, to prevent any person from engaging in any unfair labor practice (listed in section 8) affecting commerce. This power shall not be affected by any other means of adjustment or prevention that has been or may be established by agreement, law, or otherwise: *Provided,* **That the Board is empowered by agreement with any agency of any State or Territory to cede to such agency jurisdiction over any cases in any industry (other than mining, manufacturing, communications, and transportation except where predominantly local in character) even though such cases may involve labor disputes affecting commerce, unless the provision of the State or Territorial statute applicable to the determination of such cases by such agency is inconsistent with the corresponding provision of this Act or has received a construction inconsistent therewith.**

(b) Whenever it is charged that any person has engaged in or is engaging in any such unfair labor practice, the Board, or any agent or agency designated by the Board for such purposes, shall have power to issue and cause to be served upon such person a complaint stating the charges in that respect, and containing a notice of hearing before the Board or a member thereof, or before a designated agent or agency, at a place therein fixed, not less than five days after the serving of said complaint: *Provided,* **That no complaint shall issue based upon any unfair labor practice occurring more than six months prior to the filing of the charge with the Board and the service of a copy thereof upon the person against whom such charge is made, unless the person aggrieved thereby was prevented from filing such charge by reason of service in the armed forces, in which event the six-month period shall be computed from the day of his discharge.** Any such complaint may be amended by the member, agent, or agency conducting the hearing or the Board in its discretion at any time prior to the issuance of an order based thereon. The person so complained of shall have the right to file an answer to the original or amended complaint and to appear in person or otherwise and give testimony at the place and time fixed in the complaint. In the discretion of the member, agent, or agency conducting the hearing or the Board, any other person may be allowed to intervene in the said proceeding and to present testimony. [In any such proceeding the rules of evidence prevailing in courts of law or equity shall not be controlling.] **Any such proceeding shall, so far as practicable, be conducted in accordance with the rules of evidence applicable in the district courts of the United States under the rules** of civil procedure for the district courts of the United States, adopted by the Supreme Court of the United States pursuant to section 2072 of Title 28.

(c) The testimony taken by such member, agent, or agency or the Board shall be reduced to writing and filed with the Board. Thereafter, in its discretion, the Board upon notice may take further testimony or hear argument. If upon [all] **the preponderance of** the testimony taken the Board shall be of the opinion that any person named in the complaint has engaged in or is engaging in any such unfair labor practice, then the Board shall state its findings of fact and shall issue and cause to be served on such person an order requiring such person to cease and desist from such unfair labor practice, and to take such affirmative action including reinstatement of employees with or without back pay, as will effectuate the policies of this Act: *Provided,* **That where an order directs reinstatement of an employee, back pay may be required of the employer or labor organization, as the case may be, responsible for the discrimination suffered by him:** *And provided further,* **That in determining whether a complaint shall issue alleging a violation of section 8(a)(1) or section 8(a)(2), and in deciding such cases, the same regulations and rules of decision shall apply irrespective of whether or not the labor organization affected is affiliated with a labor organization national or international in scope.** Such order may further require such person to make reports from time to time showing the extent to which it has complied with the order. If upon [all] **the preponderance of** the testimony taken the Board shall not be of the opinion that the person named in the complaint has engaged in or is engaging in any such unfair labor practice, then the Board shall state its findings of fact and shall issue an order dismissing the said complaint. **No order of the Board shall require the reinstatement of any individual as an employee who has been suspended or discharged, or the payment to him of any back pay, if such individual was suspended or discharged for cause. In case the evidence is presented before a member of the Board, or before an administrative law judge or judges thereof, such member, or such judge or judges as the case may be, shall issue and cause to be served on the parties to the proceeding a proposed report, together with a recommended order, which shall be filed with the Board, and if no exceptions are filed within twenty days after service thereof upon such parties, or within such further period as the Board may authorize, such recommended order shall become the order of the Board and become effective as therein prescribed.**

(d) Until **[a transcript of]** the record in a case shall have been filed in a court, as hereinafter provided, the Board may at any time upon reasonable notice and in such manner as it shall deem proper, modify or set aside, in whole or in part, any finding or order made or issued by it.

(e) The Board shall have power to petition any [circuit] court of appeals of the United States [(including the **United States** Court of Appeals [of] **for** the District of Columbia)], or if all the [circuit] courts of appeals to which application may be made are in vacation, any district court of the United States [(including the **District** Court of the **United States for the** District of Columbia)], within any circuit or district, respectively, wherein the unfair labor practice in question occurred or wherein such person resides or transacts business, for the enforcement of such order and for appropriate temporary relief or restraining order, and shall [certify and] file in the court the record in the proceedings, *as provided in section 2112 of Title 28.* Upon [such filing] *the filing of such petition,* the court shall cause notice thereof to be served upon such person, and thereupon shall have jurisdiction of the proceeding and of the question determined therein, and shall have power to grant such temporary relief or restraining order as it deems just and proper, and to make and enter [upon the pleadings, testimony, and proceedings set forth in such transcript] a decree enforcing, modifying and enforcing as so modified, or setting aside in whole or in part the order of the Board. No objection that has not been urged before the Board, its member, agent, or agency, shall be considered by the court, unless the failure or neglect to urge such objection shall be excused because of extraordinary circumstances. The findings of the Board [as to the facts,] **with respect to questions of fact** if supported by **substantial** evidence[,] **on the record considered as a whole** shall be conclusive. If either party shall apply to the court for leave to adduce additional evidence and shall show to the satisfaction of the court that such additional evidence is material and that there were reasonable grounds for the failure to adduce such evidence in the hearing before the Board, its member, agent, or agency, the court may order such additional evidence to be taken before the Board, its member, agent, or agency, and to be made a part of the [transcript] *record.* The Board may modify its findings as to the facts, or make new findings by reason of additional evidence so taken and filed, and it shall file such modified or new findings, which **findings with respect to questions of fact** if supported by **substantial** evidence **on the record considered as a whole** shall be conclusive, and shall file its recommendations, if any, for the modification or setting aside of its original order. *Upon the filing of the record with it* the jurisdiction of the court shall be exclusive and its judgment and decree shall be final, except that the same shall be subject to review by the appropriate United States court of appeals if application was made to the district court as hereinabove provided, and by the Supreme Court of the United States upon writ of certiorari or certification as provided in section 1254 of Title 28.*

(f)*Any person aggrieved by a final order of the Board granting or denying in whole or in part the relief sought may obtain a review of such order in any United States court of appeals in the circuit wherein the unfair labor practice in question was alleged to have been engaged in or wherein such person resides or transacts business, or in the **United States** Court of Appeals [of] **for** the District of Columbia, by filing in such a court a written petition praying that the order of the Board be modified or set aside. A copy of such petition shall be forthwith [served upon the Board] *transmitted by the clerk of the court to the Board,* and thereupon the aggrieved party shall file in the court [a transcript of] the [entire] record in the proceeding, certified by the Board [including the pleading and testimony upon which the order complained of was entered and the findings and order of the Board], *as provided in section 2112 of Title 28.* Upon [such filing] *the filing of such petition,* the court shall proceed in the same manner as in the case of an application by the Board under subsection (e) of this section, and shall have the same jurisdiction to grant to the Board such temporary relief or restraining order as it deems just and proper, and in like manner to make and enter a decree enforcing, modifying, and enforcing as so modified, or setting aside in whole or in part the order of the Board; [and] the findings of the Board [as to the facts] **with respect to questions of fact** if supported by **substantial** evidence[,] **on the record considered as a whole** shall in like manner be conclusive.

(g) The commencement of proceedings under subsection (e) or (f) of this section shall not, unless specifically ordered by the court, operate as a stay of the Board's order.

(h) When granting appropriate temporary relief or a restraining order, or making and entering a decree enforcing, modifying, and enforcing as so modified or setting aside in whole or in part an order of the Board, as provided in this section, the jurisdiction of courts sitting in equity shall not be limited by the Act entitled "An Act to amend the judicial Code and to define and limit the jurisdiction of courts sitting in

---

*Sections 10(e) and 10(f) are rendered as amended by Pub. L. 85-791, §§13(b) and (c), Aug. 28, 1958, as well as by the 1947 and 1959 amendments.

equity, and for other purposes", approved March 23, 1932 (U.S.C., Supp. VII, title 29, secs. 101-115).*

(i) [Repealed.]

(j) **The Board shall have power, upon issuance of a complaint as provided in subsection (b) of this section charging that any person has engaged in or is engaging in an unfair labor practice, to petition any United States district court,** within any district wherein the unfair labor practice in question is alleged to have occurred or wherein such person resides or transacts business, for appropriate temporary relief or restraining order. Upon the filing of any such petition the court shall cause notice thereof to be served upon such person, and thereupon shall have jurisdiction to grant to the Board such temporary relief or restraining order as it deems just and proper.**

(k) **Whenever it is charged that any person has engaged in an unfair labor practice within the meaning of paragraph (4)(D) of section 8(b) of this Act, the Board is empowered and directed to hear and determine the dispute out of which such unfair labor practice shall have arisen, unless, within ten days after notice that such charge has been filed, the parties to such dispute submit to the Board satisfactory evidence that they have adjusted, or agreed upon methods for the voluntary adjustment of, the dispute. Upon compliance by the parties to the dispute with the decision of the Board or upon such voluntary adjustment of the dispute, such charge shall be dismissed.**

(*l*) **Whenever it is charged that any person has engaged in an unfair labor practice within the meaning of paragraph (4)(A), (B), or (C) of section 8(b)** *or section 8(e) or section 8(b)(7),* **the preliminary investigation of such charge shall be made forthwith and given priority over all other cases except cases of like character in the office where it is filed or to which it is referred. If, after such investigation, the officer or regional attorney to whom the matter may be referred has reasonable cause to believe such charge is true and that a complaint should issue, he shall, on behalf of the Board, petition any United States district court within any district where the unfair labor practice in question has occurred, is alleged to have occurred, or wherein such person resides or transacts business, for appropriate injunctive relief pending the final adjudication of the Board with**

---

*The Norris-LaGuardia Act of 1932.—EDS.

**Section 10(j) and subsequent sections as rendered reflect the enactment of 28 U.S.C. §132(a) and 28 U.S.C. §88, June 25, 1948, concerning the United States District Courts.

respect to such matter. Upon the filing of any such petition the district court shall have jurisdiction to grant such injunctive relief or temporary restraining order as it deems just and proper, notwithstanding any other provision of law: *Provided further,* That no temporary restraining order shall be issued without notice unless a petition alleges that substantial and irreparable injury to the charging party will be unavoidable and such temporary restraining order shall be effective for no longer than five days and will become void at the expiration of such period[.]*: Provided further, That such officer or regional attorney shall not apply for any restraining order under section 8(b)(7) if a charge against the employer under section 8(a)(2) has been filed and after the preliminary investigation, he has reasonable cause to believe that such charge is true and that a complaint should issue.* Upon filing of any such petition the courts shall cause notice thereof to be served upon any person involved in the charge and such person, including the charging party, shall be given an opportunity to appear by counsel and present any relevant testimony: *Provided further,* That for the purposes of this subsection district courts shall be deemed to have jurisdiction of a labor organization (1) in the district in which such organization maintains its principal office, or (2) in any district in which its duly authorized officers or agents are engaged in promoting or protecting the interests of employee members. The service of legal process upon such officer or agent shall constitute service upon the labor organization and make such organization a party to the suit. In situations where such relief is appropriate the procedure specified herein shall apply to charges with respect to section 8(b)(4)(D).

(m) Whenever it is charged that any person has engaged in an unfair labor practice within the meaning of subsection (a)(3) or (b)(2) of section 8, such charge shall be given priority over all other cases except cases of like character in the office where it is filed or to which it is referred and cases given priority under subsection (l) of this section.

INVESTIGATORY POWERS

§11. (§161) For the purpose of all hearings and investigations, which, in the opinion of the Board, are necessary and proper for the exercise of the powers vested in it by sections 9 and 10 —

(1) The Board, or its duly authorized agents or agencies, shall at all reasonable times have access to, for the purpose of examination, and the right to copy any evidence of any person being investigated or pro-

ceeded against that relates to any matter under investigation or in question. The Board, or any member thereof, shall upon application of any party to such proceedings, forthwith issue to such party subpenas requiring the attendance and testimony of witnesses or the production of any evidence in such proceeding or investigation requested in such application. **Within five days after the service of a subpena on any person requiring the production of any evidence in his possession or under his control, such person may petition the Board to revoke, and the Board shall revoke, such subpena if in its opinion the evidence whose production is required does not relate to any matter under investigation, or any matter in question in such proceedings, or if in its opinion such subpena does not describe with sufficient particularity the evidence whose production is required.** Any member of the Board, or any agent or agency designated by the Board for such purposes, may administer oaths and affirmations, examine witnesses, and receive evidence. Such attendance of witnesses and the production of such evidence may be required from any place in the United States or any Territory or possession thereof, at any designated place of hearing.

(2) In case of contumacy or refusal to obey a subpena issued to any person, any district court of the United States or the United States courts of any Territory or possession, within the jurisdiction of which the inquiry is carried on or within the jurisdiction of which said person guilty of contumacy or refusal to obey is found or resides or transacts business, upon application by the Board shall have jurisdiction to issue to such person an order requiring such person to appear before the Board, its member, agent, or agency, there to produce evidence if so ordered, or there to give testimony touching the matter under investigation or in question; and any failure to obey such order of the court may be punished by said court as a contempt thereof.

[(3) No person shall be excused from attending and testifying or from producing books, records, correspondence, documents, or other evidence in obedience to the subpena of the Board, on the ground that the testimony or evidence required of him may tend to incriminate him or subject him to a penalty or forfeiture; but no individual shall be prosecuted or subjected to any penalty or forfeiture for or on account of any transaction, matter, or thing concerning which he is compelled, after having claimed his privilege against self-incrimination, to testify or produce evidence, except that such individual so testifying shall not be exempt from prosecution and punishment for perjury committed in so testifying.[*]]

---

[*]Section 11(3) was repealed in 1970, by 84 Stat. 930. Similar provisions were substituted; see 18 U.S.C. §§6001, 6002, 6004 (1970).—EDS.

(4) Complaints, orders, and other process and papers of the Board, its member, agent, or agency, may be served either personally or by registered mail or by telegraph or by leaving a copy thereof at the principal office or place of business of the person required to be served. The verified return by the individual so serving the same setting forth the manner of such service shall be proof of the same, and the return post office receipt or telegraph receipt therefor when registered or certified and mailed or when telegraphed as aforesaid shall be proof of service of the same. Witnesses summoned before the Board, its member, agent, or agency, shall be paid the same fees and mileage that are paid witnesses in the courts of the United States, and witnesses whose depositions are taken and the persons taking the same shall severally be entitled to the same fees as are paid for like services in the courts of the United States.

(5) All process of any court to which application may be made under this Act may be served in the judicial district wherein the defendant or other person required to be served resides or may be found.

(6) The several departments and agencies of the Government, when directed by the President, shall furnish the Board, upon its request, all records, papers, and information in their possession relating to any matter before the Board.

§12. (§162) Any person who shall willfully resist, prevent, impede, or interfere with any member of the Board or any of its agents or agencies in the performance of duties pursuant to this Act shall be punished by a fine of not more than $5,000 or by imprisonment for not more than one year, or both.

LIMITATIONS

§13. (§163) Nothing in this Act, **except as specifically provided for herein,** shall be construed so as either to interfere with or impede or diminish in any way the right to strike, **or to affect the limitations or qualifications on that right.**

§14. (§164) **(a) Nothing herein shall prohibit any individual employed as a supervisor from becoming or remaining a member of a labor organization, but no employer subject to this Act shall be compelled to deem individuals defined herein as supervisors as employees for the purpose of any law, either national or local, relating to collective bargaining.**

(b) Nothing in this Act shall be construed as authorizing the execution or application of agreements requiring membership in a labor organization as a condition of employment in any State or Territory in which such execution or application is prohibited by State or Territorial Law.

(c)(1) The Board, in its discretion, may, by rule of decision or by published rules adopted pursuant to subchapter II of chapter 5 of Title 5,[*] *decline to assert jurisdiction over any labor dispute involving any class or category of employers, where, in the opinion of the Board, the effect of such labor dispute on commerce is not sufficiently substantial to warrant the exercise of its jurisdiction: Provided, That the Board shall not decline to assert jurisdiction over any labor dispute over which it would assert jurisdiction under the standards prevailing upon August 1, 1959.*

(2) Nothing in this Act shall be deemed to prevent or bar any agency or the courts of any State or Territory (including the Commonwealth of Puerto Rico, Guam, and the Virgin Islands), from assuming and asserting jurisdiction over labor disputes over which the Board declines, pursuant to paragraph (1) of this subsection, to assert jurisdiction.

§15. (§165) [Reference to repealed provisions of Bankruptcy Act of 1898.—EDS.]

§16. (§166) If any provision of this Act, or the application of such provision to any person or circumstances, shall be held invalid, the remainder of this Act, or the application of such provision to persons or circumstances other than those as to which it is held invalid, shall not be affected thereby.

§17. (§167) This Act may be cited as the "National Labor Relations Act".

§18. (§168) [Reference to repealed sections 9(f), (g), and (h).—EDS.]

§19. (§169) Any employee who is a member of and adheres to established and traditional tenets or teachings of a bona fide religion, body, or sect which has historically held conscientious objections to joining or financially supporting labor organizations shall not be re-

---

[*]The Administrative Procedure Act. Provision as amended by §7(b) of Pub. L. 89-544, Sept. 6, 1966.—EDS.

quired to join or financially support any labor organization as a condition of employment; except that such employee may be required in a contract between such employees' employer and a labor organization in lieu of periodic dues and initiation fees, to pay sums equal to such dues and initiation fees to a nonreligious, nonlabor organization charitable fund exempt from taxation under section 501(c)(3) of Title 26,[*] chosen by such employee from a list of at least three such funds, designated in such contract or if the contract fails to designate such funds, then to any such fund chosen by the employee. If such employee who holds conscientious objections pursuant to this section requests the labor organization to use the grievance-arbitration procedure on the employee's behalf, the labor organization is authorized to charge the employee for the reasonable cost of using such procedure.[**]

---

[*]The Internal Revenue Code.—EDS.
[**]This section was added by Pub. L. 93-360, July 26, 1974, 88 Stat. 397, and amended by Pub. L. 96-593, Dec. 24, 1980, 94 Stat. 3452.

Labor Management Relations Act of 1947[*]
61 Stat. 136 (1947), as amended, 29 U.S.C. §§141-197

Short Title and Declaration of Policy

§1. (§141) (a) This Act may be cited as the "Labor Management Relations Act, 1947."

(b) Industrial strife which interferes with the normal flow of commerce and with the full production of articles and commodities for commerce, can be avoided or substantially minimized if employers, employees, and labor organizations each recognize under law one another's legitimate rights in their relations with each other, and above all recognize under law that neither party has any right in its relations with any other to engage in acts or practices which jeopardize the public health, safety, or interest.

It is the purpose and policy of this Act, in order to promote the full flow of commerce, to prescribe the legitimate rights of both employees and employers in their relations affecting commerce, to provide orderly and peaceful procedures for preventing the interference by either with the legitimate rights of the other, to protect the rights of individual employees in their relations with labor organizations whose activities affect commerce, to define and proscribe practices on the part of labor and management which affect commerce and are inimical to the general welfare, and to protect the rights of the public in connection with labor disputes affecting commerce.

TITLE I. AMENDMENT OF NATIONAL LABOR RELATIONS ACT

§101. [The text of the National Labor Relations Act as amended is set forth supra.]

---

[*]Unless otherwise indicated, internal section references are to the NLRA or LMRA, and not to the United States Code. Provisions added by the LMRDA (1959) are in italics; provisions added by the Health Care Institutions Act (1974) are capitalized. Material deleted by the amendments is enclosed in brackets. Other amendments and deletions are specifically noted.—EDS.

TITLE II. CONCILIATION OF LABOR DISPUTES; NATIONAL EMERGENCIES

§201. (§171) It is the policy of the United States that —

(a) sound and stable industrial peace and the advancement of the general welfare, health, and safety of the Nation and of the best interests of employers and employees can most satisfactorily be secured by the settlement of issues between employers and employees through the processes of conference and collective bargaining between employers and the representatives of their employees;

(b) the settlement of issues between employers and employees through collective bargaining may be advanced by making available full and adequate government facilities for conciliation, mediation, and voluntary arbitration to aid and encourage employers and the representatives of their employees to reach and maintain agreements concerning rates of pay, hours, and working conditions, and to make all reasonable efforts to settle their differences by mutual agreement reached through conferences and collective bargaining or by such methods as may be provided for in any applicable agreement for the settlement of disputes; and

(c) certain controversies which arise between parties to collective-bargaining agreements may be avoided or minimized by making available full and adequate governmental facilities for furnishing assistance to employers and the representatives of their employees in formulating for inclusion within such agreements provision for adequate notice of any proposed changes in the terms of such agreements, for the final adjustment of grievances or questions regarding the application or interpretation of such agreements, and other provisions designed to prevent the subsequent arising of such controversies.

§202. (§172) (a) There is hereby created an independent agency to be known as the Federal Mediation and Conciliation Service (herein referred to as the "Service", except that for sixty days after June 23, 1947, such term shall refer to the Conciliation Service of the Department of Labor). The Service shall be under the direction of a Federal Mediation and Conciliation Director (hereinafter referred to as the "Director"), who shall be appointed by the President by and with the advice and consent of the Senate. The Director shall not engage in any other business, vocation, or employment.

(b) The Director is authorized, subject to the civil service laws, to appoint such clerical and other personnel as may be necessary for the execution of the functions of the Service, and shall fix their compensation in accordance with chapter 51 and subchapter III of chapter 53 of Title 5,[*] and may, without regard to the provisions of the civil service laws, appoint such conciliators and mediators as may be necessary to carry out the functions of the Service. The Director is authorized to make such expenditures for supplies, facilities, and services as he deems necessary. Such expenditures shall be allowed and paid upon presentation of itemized vouchers therefor approved by the Director or by any employee designated by him for that purpose.

(c) The principal office of the Service shall be in the District of Columbia, but the Director may establish regional offices convenient to localities in which labor controversies are likely to arise. The Director may by order, subject to revocation at any time, delegate any authority and discretion conferred upon him by this Act to any regional director, or other officer or employee of the Service. The Director may establish suitable procedures for cooperation with State and local mediation agencies. The Director shall make an annual report in writing to Congress at the end of the fiscal year.

(d) All mediation and conciliation functions of the Secretary of Labor or the United States Conciliation Service under section 51 of this title, and all functions of the United States Conciliation Service under any other law are transferred to the Federal Mediation and Conciliation Service, together with the personnel and records of the United States Conciliation Service. Such transfer shall take effect upon the sixtieth day after June 23, 1947. Such transfer shall not affect any proceedings pending before the United States Conciliation Service or any certification, order, rule, or regulation theretofore made by it or by the Secretary of Labor. The Director and the Service shall not be subject in any way to the jurisdiction or authority of the Secretary of Labor or any official or division of the Department of Labor.

Functions of the Service

§203. (§173) (a) It shall be the duty of the Service, in order to prevent or minimize interruptions of the free flow of commerce growing out of labor disputes, to assist parties to labor disputes in industries affecting commerce to settle such disputes through conciliation and mediation.

(b) The Service may proffer its services in any labor dispute in any industry affecting commerce, either upon its own motion or upon the request of one or more of the parties to the dispute, whenever in its judg-

---

[*]As amended following enactment of Pub. L. 89-554, Sept. 6, 1966, 80 Stat. 631.

ment such dispute threatens to cause a substantial interruption of commerce. The Director and the Service are directed to avoid attempting to mediate disputes which would have only a minor effect on interstate commerce if State or other conciliation services are available to the parties. Whenever the Service does proffer its services in any dispute, it shall be the duty of the Service promptly to put itself in communication with the parties and to use its best efforts, by mediation and conciliation, to bring them to agreement.

(c) If the Director is not able to bring the parties to agreement by conciliation within a reasonable time, he shall seek to induce the parties voluntarily to seek other means of settling the dispute without resort to strike, lock-out, or other coercion, including submission to the employees in the bargaining unit of the employer's last offer of settlement for approval or rejection in a secret ballot. The failure or refusal of either party to agree to any procedure suggested by the Director shall not be deemed a violation of any duty or obligation imposed by this Act.

(d) Final adjustment by a method agreed upon by the parties is declared to be the desirable method for settlement of grievance disputes arising over the application or interpretation of an existing collective-bargaining agreement. The Service is directed to make its conciliation and mediation services available in the settlement of such grievance disputes only as a last resort and in exceptional cases.

(e) The Service is authorized and directed to encourage and support the establishment and operation of joint labor management activities conducted by plant, area, and industrywide committees designed to improve labor management relationships, job security and organizational effectiveness, in accordance with the provisions of section 205A.[*]

(f) The Service may make its services available to Federal agencies to aid in the resolution of disputes under the provisions of subchapter IV of chapter 5 of Title 5. Functions performed by the Service may include assisting parties to disputes related to administrative programs, training persons in skills and procedures employed in alternative means of dispute resolution, and furnishing officers and employees of the Service to act as neutrals. Only officers and employees who are qualified in accordance with section 573 of Title 5 may be assigned to act as neutrals. The Service shall consult with the agency designated by, or the interagency committee designated or established by, the President under section 573 of Title 5 in maintaining rosters of neutrals and arbitrators, and to adopt

---

[*]Subsection (e) was added in 1978 by Pub. L. 95-524, §6(c)(1), 92 Stat. 2020.

such procedures and rules as are necessary to carry out the services authorized in this subsection.[*]

§204. (§174) (a) In order to prevent or minimize interruptions of the free flow of commerce growing out of labor disputes, employers and employees and their representatives, in any industry affecting commerce, shall —

(1) exert every reasonable effort to make and maintain agreements concerning rates of pay, hours, and working conditions, including provision for adequate notice of any proposed change in the terms of such agreements;

(2) whenever a dispute arises over the terms or application of a collective-bargaining agreement and a conference is requested by a party or prospective party thereto, arrange promptly for such a conference to be held and endeavor in such conference to settle such dispute expeditiously; and

(3) in case such dispute is not settled by conference, participate fully and promptly in such meetings as may be undertaken by the Service under this Act for the purpose of aiding in a settlement of the dispute.

§205. (§175) (a) There is created a National Labor-Management Panel which shall be composed of twelve members appointed by the President, six of whom shall be selected from among persons outstanding in the field of management and six of whom shall be selected from among persons outstanding in the field of labor. Each member shall hold office for a term of three years, except that any member appointed to fill a vacancy occurring prior to the expiration of the term for which his predecessor was appointed shall be appointed for the remainder of such term, and the terms of office of the members first taking office shall expire, as designated by the President at the time of appointment, four at the end of the first year, four at the end of the second year, and four at the end of the third year after the date of appointment. Members of the panel, when serving on business of the panel, shall be paid compensation at the rate of $25 per day, and shall also be entitled to receive an allowance for actual and necessary travel and subsistence expenses while so serving away from their places of residence.

(b) It shall be the duty of the panel, at the request of the Director, to advise in the avoidance of industrial controversies and the manner in which mediation and voluntary adjustment shall be administered, par-

---

[*]As added by §7 of Pub. L. 101-552, Nov. 15, 1990; see also Pub. L. 104-320, §9, Oct. 19, 1996.

ticularly with reference to controversies affecting the general welfare of the country.

§205A. (§175a)* (a)(1) The Service is authorized and directed to provide assistance in the establishment and operation of plant, area and industrywide labor management committees which —

(A) have been organized jointly by employers and labor organizations representing employees in that plant, area, or industry; and

(B) are established for the purpose of improving labor management relationships, job security, organizational effectiveness, enhancing economic development or involving workers in decisions affecting their jobs including improving communication with respect to subjects of mutual interest and concern.

(2) The Service is authorized and directed to enter into contracts and to make grants, where necessary or appropriate, to fulfill its responsibilities under this section.

(b)(1) No grant may be made, no contract may be entered into and no other assistance may be provided under the provisions of this section to a plant labor management committee unless the employees in that plant are represented by a labor organization and there is in effect at that plant a collective bargaining agreement.

(2) No grant may be made, no contract may be entered into and no other assistance may be provided under the provisions of this section to an area or industrywide labor management committee unless its participants include any labor organizations certified or recognized as the representative of the employees of an employer participating in such committee. Nothing in this clause shall prohibit participation in an area or industrywide committee by an employer whose employees are not represented by a labor organization.

(3) No grant may be made under the provisions of this section to any labor management committee which the Service finds to have as one of its purposes the discouragement of the exercise of rights contained in section 157 of this title, or the interference with collective bargaining in any plant, or industry.

(c) The Service shall carry out the provisions of this section through an office established for that purpose.

(d) There are authorized to be appropriated to carry out the provisions of this section $10,000,000 for the fiscal year 1979, and such sums as may be necessary thereafter.

---

*This section was added in 1978 by Pub. L. 95-524, §6(c)(2), 92 Stat. 2020.

National Emergencies

§206. (§176) Whenever in the opinion of the President of the United States, a threatened or actual strike or lock-out affecting an entire industry or a substantial part thereof engaged in trade, commerce, transportation, transmission, or communication among the several States or with foreign nations, or engaged in the production of goods for commerce, will, if permitted to occur or to continue, imperil the national health or safety, he may appoint a board of inquiry to inquire into the issues involved in the dispute and to make a written report to him within such time as he shall prescribe. Such report shall include a statement of the facts with respect to the dispute, including each party's statement of its position but shall not contain any recommendations. The President shall file a copy of such report with the Service and shall make its contents available to the public.

§207. (§177) (a) A board of inquiry shall be composed of a chairman and such other members as the President shall determine, and shall have power to sit and act in any place within the United States and to conduct such hearings either in public or in private, as it may deem necessary or proper, to ascertain the facts with respect to the causes and circumstances of the dispute.

(b) Members of a board of inquiry shall receive compensation at the rate of $50 for each day actually spent by them in the work of the board, together with necessary travel and subsistence expenses.

(c) For the purpose of any hearing or inquiry conducted by any board appointed under this title, the provisions of sections 49 and 50 of Title 15 (relating to the attendance of witnesses and the production of books, papers, and documents) are made applicable to the powers and duties of such board.

§208. (§178) (a) Upon receiving a report from a board of inquiry the President may direct the Attorney General to petition any district court of the United States having jurisdiction of the parties to enjoin such strike or lock-out or the continuing thereof, and if the court finds that such threatened or actual strike or lock-out —

(i) affects an entire industry or a substantial part thereof engaged in trade, commerce, transportation, transmission, or communication among the several States or with foreign nations, or engaged in the production of goods for commerce; and

(ii) if permitted to occur or to continue, will imperil the national health or safety, it shall have jurisdiction to enjoin any such strike or lockout, or the continuing thereof, and to make such other orders as may be appropriate.

(b) In any case, the provisions of chapter 6 of this title* shall not be applicable.

(c) The order or orders of the court shall be subject to review by the appropriate United States court of appeals and by the Supreme Court upon writ of certiorari or certification as provided in section 1254 of Title 28.

§209. (§179) (a) Whenever a district court has issued an order under section 208 enjoining acts or practices which imperil or threaten to imperil the national health or safety, it shall be the duty of the parties to the labor dispute giving rise to such order to make every effort to adjust and settle their differences, with the assistance of the Service created by this Act. Neither party shall be under any duty to accept, in whole or in part, any proposal of settlement made by the Service.

(b) Upon the issuance of such order, the President shall reconvene the board of inquiry which has previously reported with respect to the dispute. At the end of a sixty-day period (unless the dispute has been settled by that time), the board of inquiry shall report to the President the current position of the parties and the efforts which have been made for settlement, and shall include a statement by each party of its position and a statement of the employer's last offer of settlement. The President shall make such report available to the public. The National Labor Relations Board, within the succeeding fifteen days, shall take a secret ballot of the employees of each employer involved in the dispute on the question of whether they wish to accept the final offer of settlement made by their employer as stated by him and shall certify the results thereof to the Attorney General within five days thereafter.

§210. (§180) Upon the certification of the results of such ballot or upon a settlement being reached, whichever happens sooner, the Attorney General shall move the court to discharge the injunction, which motion shall then be granted and the injunction discharged. When such motion is granted, the President shall submit to the Congress a full and comprehensive report of the proceedings, including the findings of the board of inquiry and the ballot taken by the National Labor Relations Board, together with such recommendations as he may see fit to make for consideration and appropriate action.

---

*The Norris-LaGuardia Act.—Eds.

Compilation of Collective Bargaining Agreements, etc.

§211. (§181) (a) For the guidance and information of interested representatives of employers, employees, and the general public, the Bureau of Labor Statistics of the Department of Labor shall maintain a file of copies of all available collective bargaining agreements and other available agreements and actions thereunder settling or adjusting labor disputes. Such file shall be open to inspection under appropriate conditions prescribed by the Secretary of Labor, except that no specific information submitted in confidence shall be disclosed.

(b) The Bureau of Labor Statistics in the Department of Labor is authorized to furnish upon request of the Service, or employers, employees, or their representatives, all available data and factual information which may aid in the settlement of any labor dispute, except that no specific information submitted in confidence shall be disclosed.

Exemption of Railway Labor Act

§212. (§182) The provisions of this subchapter shall not be applicable with respect to any matter which is subject to the provisions of the Railway Labor Act, as amended from time to time.

Conciliation of Labor Disputes in the Health Care Industry[*]

§213. (§183) (a) If, in the opinion of the Director of the Federal Mediation and Conciliation Service, a threatened or actual strike or lockout affecting a health care institution will, if permitted to occur or to continue, substantially interrupt the delivery of health care in the locality concerned, the Director may further assist in the resolution of the impasse by establishing within 30 days after the notice to the Federal Mediation and Conciliation Service under clause (A) of the last sentence of section 8(d) (which is required by clause (3) of such section 8(d)), or within 10 days after the notice under clause (B), an impartial Board of Inquiry to investigate the issues involved in the dispute and to make a written report thereon to the parties within fifteen (15) days after the establishment of such a Board. The written report shall contain the findings of fact together with the Board's recommendations for settling the dispute, with the objective of achieving a prompt, peaceful and just settlement of the dispute. Each such Board shall be composed of such

---

[*]Added by Act of July 26, 1974, Pub. L. 93-360, §2, 88 Stat. 396.

number of individuals as the Director may deem desirable. No member appointed under this section shall have any interest or involvement in the health care institutions or the employee organizations involved in the dispute.

(b)(1) Members of any board established under this section who are otherwise employed by the Federal Government shall serve without compensation but shall be reimbursed for travel, subsistence, and other necessary expenses incurred by them in carrying out its duties under this section.

(2) Members of any board established under this section who are not subject to paragraph (1) shall receive compensation at a rate prescribed by the Director but not to exceed the daily rate prescribed for GS-18 of the General Schedule under section 5332 of Title 5, including travel for each day they are engaged in the performance of their duties under this section and shall be entitled to reimbursement for travel, subsistence, and other necessary expenses incurred by them in carrying out their duties under this section.

(c) After the establishment of a board under subsection (a) of this section and for 15 days after any such board has issued its report, no change in the status quo in effect prior to the expiration of the contract in the case of negotiations for a contract renewal, or in effect prior to the time of the impasse in the case of an initial bargaining negotiation, except by agreement, shall be made by the parties to the controversy.

(d) There are authorized to be appropriated such sums as may be necessary to carry out the provisions of this section.

TITLE III. SUITS BY AND AGAINST LABOR ORGANIZATIONS

§301. (§185) (a) Suits for violation of contracts between an employer and a labor organization representing employees in an industry affecting commerce as defined in this Act, or between any such labor organizations, may be brought in any district court of the United States having jurisdiction of the parties, without respect to the amount in controversy or without regard to the citizenship of the parties.

(b) Any labor organization which represents employees in an industry affecting commerce as defined in this Act and any employer whose activities affect commerce as defined in this Act shall be bound by the acts of its agents. Any such labor organization may sue or be sued as an entity and in behalf of the employees whom it represents in the courts of the United States. Any money judgment against a labor organization in a district court of the United States shall be enforceable only against the

organization as an entity and against its assets, and shall not be enforceable against any individual member or his assets.

(c) For the purposes of actions and proceedings by or against labor
organizations in the district courts of the United States, district courts
shall be deemed to have jurisdiction of a labor organization (1) in the
district in which such organization maintains its principal office, or (2)
in any district in which its duly authorized officers or agents are engaged in representing or acting for employee members.

(d) The service of summons, subpena, or other legal process of any
court of the United States upon an officer or agent of a labor organization, in his capacity as such, shall constitute service upon the labor organization.

(e) For the purposes of this section, in determining whether any
person is acting as an "agent" of another person so as to make such
other person responsible for his acts, the question of whether the specific acts performed were actually authorized or subsequently ratified
shall not be controlling.

Restrictions on Payments to Employee Representatives

§302. (§186) (a) It shall be unlawful for any employer *or association of employers or any person who acts as a labor relations expert,
adviser, or consultant to an employer or who acts in the interest of an
employer* to pay, *lend,* or deliver, or [to] agree to pay, *lend,* or deliver,
any money or other thing of value —

(1) to any representative of any of his employees who are employed in an industry affecting commerce[.]; *or*

*(2) to any labor organization, or any officer or employee thereof,
which represents, seeks to represent, or would admit to membership,
any of the employees of such employer who are employed in an industry affecting commerce; or*

*(3) to any employee or group or committee of employees of such
employer employed in an industry affecting commerce in excess of
their normal compensation for the purpose of causing such employee
or group or committee directly or indirectly to influence any other
employees in the exercise of the right to organize and bargain collectively through representatives of their own choosing; or*

*(4) to any officer or employee of a labor organization engaged in
an industry affecting commerce with intent to influence him in respect to any of his actions, decisions, or duties as a representative of
employees or as such officer or employee of such labor organization.*

(b)(1) It shall be unlawful for any [representative of any employees who are employed in an industry affecting commerce] *person* to *request, demand,* receive, or accept, or [to] agree to receive or accept [from the employer of such employees], *any payment, loan, or delivery of any* money or other thing of value[.] *prohibited by subsection (a) of this section.*

(2) It shall be unlawful for any labor organization, or for any person acting as an officer, agent, representative, or employee of such labor organization, to demand or accept from the operator of any motor vehicle (as defined in section 13102 of Title 49) employed in the transportation of property in commerce, or the employer of any such operator, any money or other thing of value payable to such organization or to an officer, agent, representative or employee thereof as a fee or charge for the unloading, or in connection with the unloading, of the cargo of such vehicle: Provided, That nothing in this paragraph shall be construed to make unlawful any payment by an employer to any of his employees as compensation for their services as employees.

(c) The provisions of this section shall not be applicable (1) [with] *in* respect to any money or other thing of value payable by an employer *to any of his employees whose established duties include acting openly for such employer in matters of labor relations or personnel administration or* to any representative *of his employees, or to any officer or employee of a labor organization,* who is *also* an employee or former employee of such employer, as compensation for, or by reason of, his service[s] as an employee of such employer; (2) with respect to the payment or delivery of any money or other thing of value in satisfaction of a judgment of any court or a decision or award of an arbitrator or impartial chairman or in compromise, adjustment, settlement, or release of any claim, complaint, grievance, or dispute in the absence of fraud or duress; (3) with respect to the sale or purchase of an article or commodity at the prevailing market price in the regular course of business; (4) with respect to money deducted from the wages of employees in payment of membership dues in a labor organization: *Provided,* That the employer has received from each employee, on whose account such deductions are made, a written assignment which shall not be irrevocable for a period of more than one year, or beyond the termination date of the applicable collective agreement, whichever occurs sooner; [or] (5) with respect to money or other thing of value paid to a trust fund established by such representative, for the sole and exclusive benefit of the employees of such employer, and their families and dependents (or of such employees, families, and dependents jointly with the employees of other employers making similar payments, and their families and dependents): *Provided,* That (A) such payments are held in trust for the purpose of paying, either from principal or income or both, for the benefit of employees, their families and dependents, for medical or hospital care, pensions on retirement or death of employees, compensation for injuries or illness resulting from occupational activity or insurance to provide any of the foregoing, or unemployment benefits or life insurance, disability and sickness insurance, or accident insurance; (B) the detailed basis on which such payments are to be made is specified in a written agreement with the employer, and employees and employers are equally represented in the administration of such fund, together with such neutral persons as the representatives of the employers and the representatives of [the] employees may agree upon and in the event the employer and employee groups deadlock on the administration of such fund and there are no neutral persons empowered to break such deadlock, such agreement provides that the two groups shall agree on an impartial umpire to decide such dispute, or in event of their failure to agree within a reasonable length of time, an impartial umpire to decide such dispute shall, on petition of either group, be appointed by the district court of the United States for the district where the trust fund has its principal office, and shall also contain provisions for an annual audit of the trust fund, a statement of the results of which shall be available for inspection by interested persons at the principal office of the trust fund and at such other places as may be designated in such written agreement; and (C) such payments as are intended to be used for the purpose of providing pensions or annuities for employees are made to a separate trust which provides that the funds held therein cannot be used for any purpose other than paying such pensions or annuities[.]; *or (6) with respect to money or other thing of value paid by any employer to a trust fund established by such representative for the purpose of pooled vacation, holiday, severance or similar benefits, or defraying costs of apprenticeship or other training programs: Provided, That the requirements of clause (B) of the proviso to clause (5) of this subsection shall apply to such trust funds;* (7) with respect to money or other thing of value paid by any employer to a pooled or individual trust fund established by such representative for the purpose of (A) scholarships for the benefit of employees, their families, and dependents for study at educational institutions, (B) child care centers for preschool and school age dependents of employees or (C) financial assistance for employee housing: *Provided,* That no labor organization or employer shall be required to bargain on the establishment of any such trust fund, and refusal to do so shall not constitute an unfair labor practice: *Provided further,* That the requirements of clause (B) of the proviso to clause (5) of this subsection shall apply to such trust funds; (8) with respect to money or any other thing of value paid by any employer to a trust fund established by such representative for the purpose of defraying the costs of legal services for employees, their families, and dependents for counsel or plan of their choice: *Provided,* That the requirements of clause (B) of the proviso to clause (5) of this subsection shall apply to such trust funds: *Provided further,* That no such legal services shall be furnished: (A) to initiate any proceeding directed (i) against any such employer or its officers or agents except in workman's compensation cases, or (ii) against such labor organization, or its parent or subordinate bodies, or their officers or agents, or (iii) against any other employer or labor organization, or their officers or agents, in any matter arising under the National Labor Relations Act, as amended, or this Act; and (B) in any proceeding where a labor organization would be prohibited from defraying the costs of legal services by the provisions of the Labor-Management Reporting and Disclosure Act of 1959; or (9) with respect to money or other things of value paid by an employer to a plant, area or industrywide labor management committee established for one or more of the purposes set forth in section 5(b) of the Labor Management Cooperation Act of 1978.[*]

(d)(1) Any person who participates in a transaction involving a payment, loan, or delivery of money or other thing of value to a labor organization in payment of membership dues or to a joint labor-management trust fund as defined by clause (B) of the proviso to clause (5) of subsection (c) of this section or to a plant, area, or industry-wide labor-management committee that is received and used by such labor organization, trust fund, or committee, which transaction does not satisfy all the applicable requirements of subsections (c)(4) through (c)(9) of this section, and willfully and with intent to benefit himself or to benefit other persons he knows are not permitted to receive a payment, loan, money, or other thing of value under subsections (c)(4) through (c)(9) violates this subsection, shall, upon conviction thereof, be guilty of a felony and be subject to a fine of not more than $15,000, or imprisoned for not more than five years, or both; but if the value of the amount of money or thing of value involved in any violation of the provisions of this section does not exceed $1,000, such person shall be guilty of a misdemeanor and be subject to a fine of not more than $10,000, or imprisoned for not more than one year, or both.

---

[*]Clause (7) of §302(c) was added by Pub. L. 91-96, Oct. 14, 1969, 83 Stat. 133; Clause (8) by Pub. L. 93-95, Aug. 15, 1973, 87 Stat. 314; and Clause (9) by Pub. L. 95-524, Oct. 27, 1978, 92 Stat. 2021.

(2) Except for violations involving transactions covered by subsection (d)(1) of this section, any person who willfully violates this section shall, upon conviction thereof, be guilty of a felony and be subject to a fine of not more than $15,000, or imprisoned for not more than five years, or both; but if the value of the amount of money or thing of value involved in any violation of the provisions of this section does not exceed $1,000, such person shall be guilty of a misdemeanor and be subject to a fine of not more than $10,000, or imprisoned for not more than one year, or both.[*]

(e) The district courts of the United States and the United States courts of the Territories and possessions shall have jurisdiction, for cause shown, and subject to the provisions of section 381 of Title 28 (relating to notice to opposite party) to restrain violations of this section, without regard to the provisions of section 17 of Title 15 and section 52 of this title, and the provisions of chapter 6 of this title.[**]

(f) This section shall not apply to any contract in force on June 23, 1947, until the expiration of such contract, or until July 1, 1948, whichever first occurs.

(g) Compliance with the restrictions contained in subsection (c)(5)(B) of this section upon contributions to trust funds, otherwise lawful, shall not be applicable to contributions to such trust funds established by collective agreement prior to January 1, 1946, nor shall subsection (c)(5)(A) of this section be construed as prohibiting contributions to such trust funds if prior to January 1, 1947, such funds contained provisions for pooled vacation benefits.

Unlawful Activities or Conduct

§303. (§187) (a) It shall be unlawful, for the purpose[s] of this section only, in an industry or activity affecting commerce, for any labor organization to engage in *any activity or conduct defined as an unfair labor practice in section 8(b)(4) of the National Labor Relations Act, as amended.* [, or to induce or encourage the employees of any employer to engage in, a strike or a concerted refusal in the course of their employment to use, manufacture, process, transport, or otherwise handle or work on any goods, articles, materials, or commodities or to perform any services, where an object thereof is —

(1) forcing or requiring any employer or self-employed person to join any labor or employer organization or any employer or other

---

[*]Section 302(d) was amended by Pub. L. 98-473, Oct. 12, 1984, 98 Stat. 2131.
[**]The Norris-LaGuardia Act.—EDS.

person to cease using, selling, handling, transporting, or otherwise dealing in the products of any other producer, processor, or manufacturer, or to cease doing business with any other person;

(2) forcing or requiring any other employer to recognize or bargain with a labor organization as the representative of his employees unless such labor organization has been certified as the representative of such employees under the provisions of section 9 of the National Labor Relations Act;

(3) forcing or requiring any employer to recognize or bargain with a particular labor organization as the representative of his employees if another labor organization has been certified as the representative of such employees under the provisions of section 9 of the National Labor Relations Act;

(4) forcing or requiring any employer to assign particular work to employees in a particular labor organization or in a particular trade, craft, or class rather than to employees in another labor organization or in another trade, craft, or class unless such employer is failing to conform to an order or certification of the National Labor Relations Board determining the bargaining representative for employees performing such work. Nothing contained in this subsection shall be construed to make unlawful a refusal by any person to enter upon the premises of any employer (other than his own employer), if the employees of such employer are engaged in a strike ratified or approved by a representative of such employees whom such employer is required to recognize under the National Labor Relations Act.]

(b) Whoever shall be injured in his business or property by reason or (sic) any violation of subsection (a) may sue therefor in any district court of the United States subject to the limitations and provisions of section 301 hereof without respect to the amount in controversy, or in any other court having jurisdiction of the parties, and shall recover the damages by him sustained and the cost of the suit.

Restriction on Political Contributions

[Section 304 of the LMRA was repealed and reenacted in other statutes, first in 1948 and then in the 1976 Federal Election Campaign Act. The relevant parts of that Act, as amended in 1980, are reprinted below.—EDS.]

Contributions or Expenditures by National Banks, Corporations, or Labor Organizations

§316. (2 U.S.C. §441b) (a) It is unlawful for any national bank, or any corporation organized by authority of any law of Congress, to make a contribution or expenditure in connection with any election to any political office, or in connection with any primary election or political convention or caucus held to select candidates for any political office, or for any corporation whatever, or any labor organization, to make a contribution or expenditure in connection with any election at which presidential and vice presidential electors or a Senator or Representative in, or a Delegate or Resident Commissioner to, Congress are to be voted for, or in connection with any primary election or political convention or caucus held to select candidates for any of the foregoing offices, or for any candidate, political committee, or other person knowingly to accept or receive any contribution prohibited by this section, or any officer or any director of any corporation or any national bank or any officer of any labor organization to consent to any contribution or expenditure by the corporation, national bank, or labor organization, as the case may be, prohibited by this section.

(b)(1) For the purposes of this section the term "labor organization" means any organization of any kind, or any agency or employee representation committee or plan, in which employees participate and which exists for the purpose, in whole or in part, of dealing with employers concerning grievances, labor disputes, wages, rates of pay, hours of employment, or conditions of work.

(2) For purposes of this section and section 79l(h) of Title 15, the term "contribution or expenditure" shall include any direct or indirect payment, distribution, loan, advance, deposit, or gift of money, or any services, or anything of value (except a loan of money by a national or State bank made in accordance with the applicable banking laws and regulations and in the ordinary course of business) to any candidate, campaign committee, or political party or organization, in connection with any election to any of the offices referred to in this section, but shall not include (A) communications by a corporation to its stockholders and executive or administrative personnel and their families or by a labor organization to its members and their families on any subject; (B) nonpartisan registration and get-out-the-vote campaigns by a corporation aimed at its stockholders and executive or administrative personnel and their families, or by a labor organization aimed at its members and their families; and (C) the establishment, administration, and solicitation of contributions to a separate

segregated fund to be utilized for political purposes by a corporation, labor organization, membership organization, cooperative, or corporation without capital stock.

(3) It shall be unlawful —

(A) for such a fund to make a contribution or expenditure by utilizing money on anything of value secured by physical force, job discrimination, financial reprisals, or the threat of force, job discrimination, or financial reprisal; or by dues, fees, or other moneys required as a condition of membership in a labor organization or as a condition of employment, or by moneys obtained in any commercial transaction;

(B) for any person soliciting an employee for a contribution to such a fund to fail to inform such employee of the political purposes of such fund at the time of such solicitation; and

(C) for any person soliciting an employee for a contribution to such a fund to fail to inform such employee, at the time of such solicitation, of his right to refuse to so contribute without any reprisal.

(4)(A) Except as provided in subparagraphs (B), (C), and (D), it shall be unlawful —

(i) for a corporation, or a separate segregated fund established by a corporation, to solicit contributions to such a fund from any person other than its stockholders and their families and its executive or administrative personnel and their families, and

(ii) for a labor organization, or a separate segregated fund established by a labor organization, to solicit contributions to such a fund from any person other than its members and their families.

(B) It shall not be unlawful under this section for a corporation, a labor organization, or a separate segregated fund established by such corporation or such labor organization, to make 2 written solicitations for contributions during the calendar year from any stockholder, executive or administrative personnel, or employee of a corporation or the families of such persons. A solicitation under this subparagraph may be made only by mail addressed to stockholders, executive or administrative personnel, or employees at their residence and shall be so designed that the corporation, labor organization, or separate segregated fund conducting such solicitation cannot determine who makes a contribution of $50 or less as a result of such solicitation and who does not make such a contribution.

(C) This paragraph shall not prevent a membership organization, cooperative, or corporation without capital stock, or a separate segregated fund established by a membership organization, cooperative, or corporation without capital stock, from soliciting contributions to such a fund from members of such organization, cooperative, or corporation without capital stock.

(D) This paragraph shall not prevent a trade association or a separate segregated fund established by a trade association from soliciting contributions from the stockholders and executive or administrative personnel of the member corporations of such trade association and the families of such stockholders or personnel to the extent that such solicitation of such stockholders and personnel, and their families, has been separately and specifically approved by the member corporation involved, and such member corporation does not approve any such solicitation by more than one such trade association in any calendar year.

(5) Notwithstanding any other law, any method of soliciting voluntary contributions or of facilitating the making of voluntary contributions to a separate segregated fund established by a corporation, permitted by law to corporations with regard to stockholders and executive or administrative personnel, shall also be permitted to labor organizations with regard to their members.

(6) Any corporation, including its subsidiaries, branches, divisions, and affiliates, that utilizes a method of soliciting voluntary contributions or facilitating the making of voluntary contributions, shall make available such method, on written request and at a cost sufficient only to reimburse the corporation for the expenses incurred thereby, to a labor organization representing any members working for such corporation, its subsidiaries, branches, divisions, and affiliates.

(7) For purposes of this section, the term "executive or administrative personnel" means individuals employed by a corporation who are paid on a salary, rather than hourly, basis and who have policy-making, managerial, professional, or supervisory responsibilities.

Strikes by Government Employees [Repealed]*

[§305. (§188) It shall be unlawful for any individual employed by the United States or any agency thereof including wholly owned Government corporations to participate in any strike. Any individual employed by the United States or by any such agency who strikes shall be discharged immediately from his employment, and shall forfeit his civil-service status, if any, and shall not be eligible for reemployment for three years by the United States or any such agency.]

TITLE IV. CREATION OF JOINT COMMITTEE TO STUDY AND REPORT ON BASIC PROBLEMS AFFECTING FRIENDLY LABOR RELATIONS AND PRODUCTIVITY

[Text omitted.]

TITLE V. DEFINITIONS

§501. (§142) When used in this Act —

(1) The term "industry affecting commerce" means any industry or activity in commerce or in which a labor dispute would burden or obstruct commerce or tend to burden or obstruct commerce or the free flow of commerce.

(2) The term "strike" includes any strike or other concerted stoppage of work by employees (including a stoppage by reason of the expiration of a collective-bargaining agreement) and any concerted slowdown or other concerted interruption of operations by employees.

(3) The terms "commerce", "labor disputes", "employer", "employee", "labor organization", "representative", "person", and "supervisor" shall have the same meaning as when used in the National Labor Relations Act as amended by this Act.

---

*Section 305 was repealed by Act of Aug. 9, 1955, c.690, §4(3), 69 Stat. 625. Congress instead enacted 5 U.S.C. §§118p-118r (now 5 U.S.C. §§3333, 7311; 18 U.S.C. §1918). Those provisions make strikes by federal employees a felony. The Civil Service Reform Act of 1978 also makes strikes and other work stoppages by federal employees unfair labor practices (5 U.S.C. §§7116(b)(7)(A) and (B)), and provides for decertification of unions that strike (5 U.S.C. §7120(f)).—EDS.

Saving Provisions

§502. (§143) Nothing in this Act shall be construed to require an individual employee to render labor or service without his consent, nor shall anything in this Act be construed to make the quitting of his labor by an individual employee an illegal act; nor shall any court issue any process to compel the performance by an individual employee of such labor or service, without his consent; nor shall the quitting of labor by an employee or employees in good faith because of abnormally dangerous conditions for work at the place of employment of such employee or employees be deemed a strike under this Act.

Separability

§503. (§144) If any provision of this Act, or the application of such provision to any person or circumstance, shall be held invalid, the remainder of this Act, or the application of such provision to persons or circumstances other than those as to which it is held invalid, shall not be affected thereby.

Labor-Management Reporting and Disclosure Act of 1959
73 Stat. 519 (1959), as amended, 29 U.S.C. §§401-531

§2. (§401) Congressional declaration of findings, purposes, and policy

(a) *Standards for labor-management relations.* The Congress finds that, in the public interest, it continues to be the responsibility of the Federal Government to protect employees' rights to organize, choose their own representatives, bargain collectively, and otherwise engage in concerted activities for their mutual aid or protection; that the relations between employers and labor organizations and the millions of workers they represent have a substantial impact on the commerce of the Nation; and that in order to accomplish the objective of a free flow of commerce it is essential that labor organizations, employers, and their officials adhere to the highest standards of responsibility and ethical conduct in administering the affairs of their organizations, particularly as they affect labor-management relations.

(b) *Protection of rights of employees and the public.* The Congress further finds, from recent investigations in the labor and management fields, that there have been a number of instances of breach of trust, corruption, disregard of the rights of individual employees, and other failures to observe high standards of responsibility and ethical conduct which require further and supplementary legislation that will afford necessary protection of the rights and interests of employees and the public generally as they relate to the activities of labor organizations, employers, labor relations consultants, and their officers and representatives.

(c) *Necessity to eliminate or prevent improper practices.* The Congress, therefore, further finds and declares that the enactment of this chapter is necessary to eliminate or prevent improper practices on the part of labor organizations, employers, labor relations consultants, and their officers and representatives which distort and defeat the policies of the Labor Management Relations Act, 1947, as amended [29 U.S.C. §141 et seq.], and the Railway Labor Act, as amended [45 U.S.C. §151 et seq.], and have the tendency or necessary effect of burdening or obstructing commerce by (1) impairing the efficiency, safety, or operation of the instrumentalities of commerce; (2) occurring in the current of commerce; (3) materially affecting, restraining, or controlling the flow of raw materials or manufactured or processed goods into or from the channels of commerce, or the prices of such materials or goods in commerce; or (4) causing diminution of employment and wages in such volume as substantially to impair or disrupt the market for goods flowing into or from the channels of commerce.

§3. (§402) Definitions

For the purposes of this chapter —

(a) "Commerce" means trade, traffic, commerce, transportation, transmission, or communication among the several States or between any State and any place outside thereof.

(b) "State" includes any State of the United States, the District of Columbia, Puerto Rico, the Virgin Islands, American Samoa, Guam, Wake Island, the Canal Zone, and Outer Continental Shelf lands defined in the Outer Continental Shelf Lands Act [43 U.S.C. §1331 et seq.].

(c) "Industry affecting commerce" means any activity, business, or industry in commerce or in which a labor dispute would hinder or obstruct commerce or the free flow of commerce and includes any activity or industry "affecting commerce" within the meaning of the Labor Management Relations Act, 1947, as amended [29 U.S.C. §141 et seq.], or the Railway Labor Act, as amended [45 U.S.C. §151 et seq.].

(d) "Person" includes one or more individuals, labor organizations, partnerships, associations, corporations, legal representatives, mutual companies, joint-stock companies, trusts, unincorporated organizations, trustees, trustees in cases under title 11, or receivers.

(e) "Employer" means any employer or any group or association of employers engaged in an industry affecting commerce (1) which is, with respect to employees engaged in an industry affecting commerce, an employer within the meaning of any law of the United States relating to the employment of any employees or (2) which may deal with any labor organization concerning grievances, labor disputes, wages, rates of pay, hours of employment, or conditions of work, and includes any person acting directly or indirectly as an employer or as an agent of an employer in relation to an employee but does not include the United States or any corporation wholly owned by the Government of the United States or any State or political subdivision thereof.

(f) "Employee" means any individual employed by an employer, and includes any individual whose work has ceased as a consequence of, or in connection with, any current labor dispute or because of any unfair labor practice or because of exclusion or expulsion from a labor organization in any manner or for any reason inconsistent with the requirements of this chapter.

(g) "Labor dispute" includes any controversy concerning terms, tenure, or conditions of employment, or concerning the association or representation of persons in negotiating, fixing, maintaining, changing, or seeking to arrange terms or conditions of employment, regardless of whether the disputants stand in the proximate relation of employer and employee.

(h) "Trusteeship" means any receivership, trusteeship, or other method of supervision or control whereby a labor organization suspends the autonomy otherwise available to a subordinate body under its constitution or bylaws.

(i) "Labor organization" means a labor organization engaged in an industry affecting commerce and includes any organization of any kind, any agency, or employee representation committee, group, association, or plan so engaged in which employees participate and which exists for the purpose, in whole or in part, of dealing with employers concerning grievances, labor disputes, wages, rates of pay, hours, or other terms or conditions of employment, and any conference, general committee, joint or system board, or joint council so engaged which is subordinate to a national or international labor organization, other than a State or local central body.

(j) A labor organization shall be deemed to be engaged in an industry affecting commerce if it —

(1) is the certified representative of employees under the provisions of the National Labor Relations Act, as amended [29 U.S.C. §151 et seq.], or the Railway Labor Act, as amended [45 U.S.C. §151 et seq.]; or

(2) although not certified, is a national or international labor organization or a local labor organization recognized or acting as the representative of employees of an employer or employers engaged in an industry affecting commerce; or

(3) has chartered a local labor organization or subsidiary body which is representing or actively seeking to represent employees of employers within the meaning of paragraph (1) or (2); or

(4) has been chartered by a labor organization representing or actively seeking to represent employees within the meaning of paragraph (1) or (2) as the local or subordinate body through which such employees may enjoy membership or become affiliated with such labor organization; or

(5) is a conference, general committee, joint or system board, or joint council, subordinate to a national or international labor organization, which includes a labor organization engaged in an industry

affecting commerce within the meaning of any of the preceding paragraphs of this subsection, other than a State or local central body.

(k) "Secret ballot" means the expression by ballot, voting machine, or otherwise, but in no event by proxy, of a choice with respect to any election or vote taken upon any matter, which is cast in such a manner that the person expressing such choice cannot be identified with the choice expressed.

(*l*) "Trust in which a labor organization is interested" means a trust or other fund or organization (1) which was created or established by a labor organization, or one or more of the trustees or one or more members of the governing body of which is selected or appointed by a labor organization, and (2) a primary purpose of which is to provide benefits for the members of such labor organization or their beneficiaries.

(m) "Labor relations consultant" means any person who, for compensation, advises or represents an employer, employer organization, or labor organization concerning employee organizing, concerted activities, or collective bargaining activities.

(n) "Officer" means any constitutional officer, any person authorized to perform the functions of president, vice president, secretary, treasurer, or other executive functions of a labor organization, and any member of its executive board or similar governing body.

(*o*) "Member" or "member in good standing", when used in reference to a labor organization, includes any person who has fulfilled the requirements for membership in such organization, and who neither has voluntarily withdrawn from membership nor has been expelled or suspended from membership after appropriate proceedings consistent with lawful provisions of the constitution and bylaws of such organization.

(p) "Secretary" means the Secretary of Labor.

(q) "Officer, agent, shop steward, or other representative," when used with respect to a labor organization, includes elected officials and key administrative personnel, whether elected or appointed (such as business agents, heads of departments or major units, and organizers who exercise substantial independent authority), but does not include salaried nonsupervisory professional staff, stenographic, and service personnel.

(r) "District court of the United States" means a United States district court and a United States court of any place subject to the jurisdiction of the United States.

TITLE I. BILL OF RIGHTS OF MEMBERS OF LABOR ORGANIZATION

§101. (§411) Bill of rights; constitution and bylaws of labor organizations

(a)(1) *Equal rights.* Every member of a labor organization shall have equal rights and privileges within such organization to nominate candidates, to vote in elections or referendums of the labor organization, to attend membership meetings, and to participate in the deliberations and voting upon the business of such meetings, subject to reasonable rules and regulations in such organization's constitution and bylaws.

(2) *Freedom of speech and assembly.* Every member of any labor organization shall have the right to meet and assemble freely with other members; and to express any views, arguments, or opinions; and to express at meetings of the labor organization his views, upon candidates in an election of the labor organization or upon any business properly before the meeting, subject to the organization's established and reasonable rules pertaining to the conduct of meetings: *Provided,* That nothing herein shall be construed to impair the right of a labor organization to adopt and enforce reasonable rules as to the responsibility of every member toward the organization as an institution and to his refraining from conduct that would interfere with its performance of its legal or contractual obligations.

(3) *Dues, initiation fees, and assessments.* Except in the case of a federation of national or international labor organizations, the rates of dues and initiation fees payable by members of any labor organization in effect on September 14, 1959 shall not be increased, and no general or special assessment shall be levied upon such members, except —

(A) in the case of a local labor organization, (i) by majority vote by secret ballot of the members in good standing voting at a general or special membership meeting, after reasonable notice of the intention to vote upon such question, or (ii) by majority vote of the members in good standing voting in a membership referendum conducted by secret ballot; or

(B) in the case of a labor organization, other than a local labor organization or a federation of national or international labor organizations, (i) by majority vote of the delegates voting at a regular convention, or at a special convention of such labor organization held upon not less than thirty days' written notice to the principal office of each local or constituent labor organization entitled to such notice, or (ii) by majority vote of the members in good standing of such labor organization voting in a membership referendum conducted by secret ballot, or (iii) by majority vote of the members of the executive board or similar governing body of such labor organization, pursuant to express authority contained in the constitution and bylaws of such labor organization: *Provided,* That any such action on the part of the executive board or similar governing body shall be effective only until the next regular convention of such labor organization.

(4) *Protection of the right to sue.* No labor organization shall limit the right of any member thereof to institute an action in any court, or in a proceeding before any administrative agency, irrespective of whether or not the labor organization or its officers are named as defendants or respondents in such action or proceeding, or the right of any member of a labor organization to appear as a witness in any judicial, administrative, or legislative proceeding, or to petition any legislature or to communicate with any legislator: *Provided,* That such member may be required to exhaust reasonable hearing procedures (but not to exceed a four-month lapse of time) within such organization, before instituting legal or administrative proceedings against such organizations or any officer thereof: *And provided further,* That no interested employer or employer association shall directly or indirectly finance, encourage, or participate in, except as a party, any such action, proceeding, appearance, or petition.

(5) *Safeguards against improper disciplinary action.* No member of any labor organization may be fined, suspended, expelled, or otherwise disciplined except for nonpayment of dues by such organization or by any officer thereof unless such member has been (A) served with written specific charges; (B) given a reasonable time to prepare his defense; (C) afforded a full and fair hearing.

(b) *Invalidity of constitution and bylaws.* Any provision of the constitution and bylaws of any labor organization which is inconsistent with the provisions of this section shall be of no force or effect.

§102. (§412) Civil action for infringement of rights; jurisdiction

Any person whose rights secured by the provisions of this subchapter have been infringed by any violation of this subchapter may bring a civil action in a district court of the United States for such relief (including injunctions) as may be appropriate. Any such action against a labor organization shall be brought in the district court of the United States for the district where the alleged violation occurred, or where the principal office of such labor organization is located.

§103. (§413) Retention of existing rights of members

Nothing contained in this subchapter shall limit the rights and remedies of any member of a labor organization under any State or Federal law or before any court or other tribunal, or under the constitution and bylaws of any labor organization.

§104. (§414) Right to copies of collective bargaining agreements

It shall be the duty of the secretary or corresponding principal officer of each labor organization, in the case of a local labor organization, to forward a copy of each collective bargaining agreement made by such labor organization with any employer to any employee who requests such a copy and whose rights as such employee are directly affected by such agreement, and in the case of a labor organization other than a local labor organization, to forward a copy of any such agreement to each constituent unit which has members directly affected by such agreement; and such officer shall maintain at the principal office of the labor organization of which he is an officer copies of any such agreement made or received by such labor organization, which copies shall be available for inspection by any member or by any employee whose rights are affected by such agreement. The provisions of section 440 of this title shall be applicable in the enforcement of this section.

§105. (§415) Information to members of provisions of chapter

Every labor organization shall inform its members concerning the provisions of this chapter.

Title II. Reporting by Labor Organizations, Officers and Employees of Labor Organizations, and Employers

§201. (§431) Report of labor organizations

(a) *Adoption and filing of constitution and bylaws; contents of report.* Every labor organization shall adopt a constitution and bylaws and shall file a copy thereof with the Secretary, together with a report, signed by its president and secretary or corresponding principal officers, containing the following information —

(1) the name of the labor organization, its mailing address, and any other address at which it maintains its principal office or at which it keeps the records referred to in this subchapter;

(2) the name and title of each of its officers;

(3) the initiation fee or fees required from a new or transferred member and fees for work permits required by the reporting labor organization;

(4) the regular dues or fees or other periodic payments required to remain a member of the reporting labor organization; and

(5) detailed statements, or references to specific provisions of documents filed under this subsection which contain such statements, showing the provision made and procedures followed with respect to each of the following: (A) qualifications for or restrictions on membership, (B) levying of assessments, (C) participation in insurance or other benefit plans, (D) authorization for disbursement of funds of the labor organization, (E) audit of financial transactions of the labor organization, (F) the calling of regular and special meetings, (G) the selection of officers and stewards and of any representatives to other bodies composed of labor organizations' representatives, with a specific statement of the manner in which each officer was elected, appointed, or otherwise selected, (H) discipline or removal of officers or agents for breaches of their trust, (1) imposition of fines, suspensions, and expulsions of members, including the grounds for such action and any provision made for notice, hearing, judgment on the evidence, and appeal procedures, (J) authorization for bargaining demands, (K) ratification of contract terms, (L) authorization for strikes, and (M) issuance of work permits. Any change in the information required by this subsection shall be reported to the Secretary at the time the reporting labor organization files with the Secretary the annual financial report required by subsection (b) of this section.

(b) *Annual financial report; filing; contents.* Every labor organization shall file annually with the Secretary a financial report signed by its president and treasurer or corresponding principal officers containing the following information in such detail as may be necessary accurately to disclose its financial condition and operations for its preceding fiscal year —

(1) assets and liabilities at the beginning and end of the fiscal year;

(2) receipts of any kind and the sources thereof;

(3) salary, allowances, and other direct or indirect disbursements (including reimbursed expenses) to each officer and also to each employee who, during such fiscal year, received more than $10,000 in the aggregate from such labor organization and any other labor organization affiliated with it or with which it is affiliated, or which is affiliated with the same national or international labor organization;

(4) direct and indirect loans made to any officer, employee, or member, which aggregated more than $250 during the fiscal year, together with a statement of the purpose, security, if any, and arrangements for repayment;

(5) direct and indirect loans to any business enterprise, together with a statement of the purpose, security, if any, and arrangements for repayment; and

(6) other disbursements made by it including the purposes thereof, all in such categories as the Secretary may prescribe.

(c) *Availability of information to members; examination of books, records, and accounts.* Every labor organization required to submit a report under this subchapter shall make available the information required to be contained in such report to all of its members, and every such labor organization and its officers shall be under a duty enforceable at the suit of any member of such organization in any State court of competent jurisdiction or in the district court of the United States for the district in which such labor organization maintains its principal office, to permit such member for just cause to examine any books, records, and accounts necessary to verify such report. The court in such action may, in its discretion, in addition to any judgment awarded to the plaintiff or plaintiffs, allow a reasonable attorney's fee to be paid by the defendant, and costs of the action.

§202. (§432) Report of officers and employees of labor organizations

(a) *Filing; contents of report.* Every officer of a labor organization and every employee of a labor organization (other than an employee performing exclusively clerical or custodial services) shall file with the

Secretary a signed report listing and describing for his preceding fiscal year —

(1) any stock, bond, security, or other interest, legal or equitable, which he or his spouse or minor child directly or indirectly held in, and any income or any other benefit with monetary value (including reimbursed expenses) which he or his spouse or minor child derived directly or indirectly from, an employer whose employees such labor organization represents or is actively seeking to represent, except payments and other benefits received as a bona fide employee of such employer;

(2) any transaction in which he or his spouse or minor child engaged, directly or indirectly, involving any stock, bond, security, or loan to or from, or other legal or equitable interest in the business of an employer whose employees such labor organization represents or is actively seeking to represent;

(3) any stock, bond, security, or other interest, legal or equitable, which he or his spouse or minor child directly or indirectly held in, and any income or any other benefit with monetary value (including reimbursed expenses) which he or his spouse or minor child directly or indirectly derived from, any business a substantial part of which consists of buying from, selling or leasing to, or otherwise dealing with, the business of an employer whose employees such labor organization represents or is actively seeking to represent;

(4) any stock, bond, security, or other interest, legal or equitable, which he or his spouse or minor child directly or indirectly held in, and any income or any other benefit with monetary value (including reimbursed expenses) which he or his spouse or minor child directly or indirectly derived from, a business any part of which consists of buying from, or selling or leasing directly or indirectly to, or otherwise dealing with such labor organization;

(5) any direct or indirect business transaction or arrangement between him or his spouse or minor child and any employer whose employees his organization represents or is actively seeking to represent, except work performed and payments and benefits received as a bona fide employee of such employer and except purchases and sales of goods or services in the regular course of business at prices generally available to any employee of such employer; and

(6) any payment of money or other thing of value (including reimbursed expenses) which he or his spouse or minor child received directly or indirectly from any employer or any person who acts as a

labor relations consultant to an employer, except payments of the kinds referred to in section 186(c) of this title.

(b) *Report of certain bona fide investments.* The provisions of paragraphs (1), (2), (3), (4), and (5) of subsection (a) of this section shall not be construed to require any such officer or employee to report his bona fide investments in securities traded on a securities exchange registered as a national securities exchange under the Securities Exchange Act of 1934 [15 U.S.C. §78a et seq.], in shares in an investment company registered under the Investment Company Act of 1940 [15 U.S.C. §80a-1 et seq.], or in securities of a public utility holding company registered under the Public Utility Holding Company Act of 1935 [15 U.S.C. §79 et seq.], or to report any income derived therefrom.

(c) *Exemption from filing requirement.* Nothing contained in this section shall be construed to require any officer or employee of a labor organization to file a report under subsection (a) of this section unless he or his spouse or minor child holds or has held an interest, has received income or any other benefit with monetary value or a loan, or has engaged in a transaction described therein.

§203. (§433) Report of employers

(a) *Filing and contents of report of payments, loans, promises, agreements, or arrangements.* Every employer who in any fiscal year made —

(1) any payment or loan, direct or indirect, of money or other thing of value (including reimbursed expenses), or any promise or agreement therefor, to any labor organization or officer, agent, shop steward, or other representative of a labor organization, or employee of any labor organization, except (A) payments or loans made by any national or State bank, credit union, insurance company, savings and loan association or other credit institution and (B) payments of the kind referred to in section 186(c) of this title;

(2) any payment (including reimbursed expenses) to any of his employees, or any group or committee of such employees, for the purpose of causing such employee or group or committee of employees to persuade other employees to exercise or not to exercise, or as the manner of exercising, the right to organize and bargain collectively through representatives of their own choosing unless such payments were contemporaneously or previously disclosed to such other employees;

(3) any expenditure, during the fiscal year, where an object thereof, directly or indirectly, is to interfere with, restrain, or coerce employees in the exercise of the right to organize and bargain collectively through representatives of their own choosing, or is to obtain information concerning the activities of employees or a labor organization in connection with a labor dispute involving such employer, except for use solely in conjunction with an administrative or arbitral proceeding or a criminal or civil judicial proceeding;

(4) any agreement or arrangement with a labor relations consultant or other independent contractor or organization pursuant to which such person undertakes activities where an object thereof, directly or indirectly, is to persuade employees to exercise or not to exercise, or persuade employees as to the manner of exercising, the right to organize and bargain collectively through representatives of their own choosing, or undertakes to supply such employer with information concerning the activities of employees or a labor organization in connection with a labor dispute involving such employer, except information for use solely in conjunction with an administrative or arbitral proceeding or a criminal or civil judicial proceeding; or

(5) any payment (including reimbursed expenses) pursuant to an agreement or arrangement described in subdivision (4);

shall file with the Secretary a report, in a form prescribed by him, signed by its president and treasurer or corresponding principal officers showing in detail the date and amount of each such payment, loan, promise, agreement, or arrangement and the name, address, and position, if any, in any firm or labor organization of the person to whom it was made and a full explanation of the circumstances of all such payments, including the terms of any agreement or understanding pursuant to which they were made.

(b) *Persuasive activities relating to the fight to organize and bargain collectively; supplying information of activities in connection with labor disputes; filing and contents of report of agreement or arrangement.* Every person who pursuant to any agreement or arrangement with an employer undertakes activities where an object thereof is, directly or indirectly —

(1) to persuade employees to exercise or not to exercise, or persuade employees as to the manner of exercising, the right to organize and bargain collectively through representatives of their own choosing; or

(2) to supply an employer with information concerning the activities of employees or a labor organization in connection with a labor dispute involving such employer, except information for use solely in

conjunction with an administrative or arbitral proceeding or a criminal or civil judicial proceeding;

shall file within thirty days after entering into such agreement or arrangement a report with the Secretary, signed by its president and treasurer or corresponding principal officers, containing the name under which such person is engaged in doing business and the address of its principal office, and a detailed statement of the terms and conditions of such agreement or arrangement. Every such person shall file annually, with respect to each fiscal year during which payments were made as a result of such an agreement or arrangement, a report with the Secretary, signed by its president and treasurer or corresponding principal officers, containing a statement (A) of its receipts of any kind from employers on account of labor relations advice or services, designating the sources thereof, and (B) of its disbursements of any kind, in connection with such services and the purposes thereof. In each such case such information shall be set forth in such categories as the Secretary may prescribe.

(c) *Advisory or representative services exempt from filing requirements.* Nothing in this section shall be construed to require any employer or other person to file a report covering the services of such person by reason of his giving or agreeing to give advice to such employer or representing or agreeing to represent such employer before any court, administrative agency, or tribunal of arbitration or engaging or agreeing to engage in collective bargaining on behalf of such employer with respect to wages, hours, or other terms or conditions of employment or the negotiation of an agreement or any question arising thereunder.

(d) *Exemption from filing requirements generally.* Nothing contained in this section shall be construed to require an employer to file a report under subsection (a) of this section unless he has made an expenditure, payment, loan, agreement, or arrangement of the kind described therein. Nothing contained in this section shall be construed to require any other person to file a report under subsection (b) of this section unless he was a party to an agreement or arrangement of the kind described therein.

(e) *Services by and payments to regular officers, supervisors, and employees of employer.* Nothing contained in this section shall be construed to require any regular officer, supervisor, or employee of an employer to file a report in connection with services rendered to such employer nor shall any employer be required to file a report covering expenditures made to any regular officer, supervisor, or employee of an employer as compensation for service as a regular officer, supervisor, or employee of such employer.

(f) *Rights protected by section 158(c) of this title.* Nothing contained in this section shall be construed as an amendment to, or modification of the rights protected by, section 158(c) of this title.

(g) *Definition.* The term "interfere with, restrain, or coerce" as used in this section means interference, restraint, and coercion which, if done with respect to the exercise of rights guaranteed in section 157 of this title, would, under section 158(a) of this title, constitute an unfair labor practice.

§204. (§434) Exemption of attorney-client communications

Nothing contained in this chapter shall be construed to require an attorney who is a member in good standing of the bar of any State, to include in any report required to be filed pursuant to the provisions of this chapter any information which was lawfully communicated to such attorney by any of his clients in the course of a legitimate attorney-client relationship.

§205. (§435) Reports and documents as public information

(a) *Publication; statistical and research purposes.* The contents of the reports and documents filed with the Secretary pursuant to sections 431, 432, 433, and 441 of this title shall be public information, and the Secretary may publish any information and data which he obtains pursuant to the provisions of this subchapter. The Secretary may use the information and data for statistical and research purposes, and compile and publish such studies, analyses, reports, and surveys based thereon as he may deem appropriate.

(b) *Inspection and examination of information and data.* The Secretary shall by regulation make reasonable provision for the inspection and examination, on the request of any person, of the information and data contained in any report or other document filed with him pursuant to section 431, 432, 433, or 441, of this title.

(c) *Copies of reports or documents; availability to State agencies.* The Secretary shall by regulation provide for the furnishing by the Department of Labor of copies of reports or other documents filed with the Secretary pursuant to this subchapter, upon payment of a charge based upon the cost of the service. The Secretary shall make available without payment of a charge, or require any person to furnish, to such State agency as is designated by law or by the Governor of the State in which such person has his principal place of business or headquarters, upon request of the Governor of such State, copies of any reports and documents filed by such person with the Secretary pursuant to section 431, 432, 433, or 441 of this title, or of information and data contained therein. No person shall be required by reason of any law of any State to furnish to any officer or agency of such State any information included in a report filed by such person with the Secretary pursuant to the provisions of this subchapter, if a copy of such report, or of the portion thereof containing such information, is furnished to such officer or agency. All moneys received in payment of such charges fixed by the Secretary pursuant to this subsection shall be deposited in the general fund of the Treasury.

§206. (§436) Retention of records

Every person required to file any report under this Subchapter shall maintain records of the matters required to be reported which will provide in sufficient detail the necessary basic information and data from which the documents filed with the Secretary may be verified, explained, or clarified, and checked for accuracy and completeness, and shall include vouchers, worksheets, receipts, and applicable resolutions, and shall keep such records available for examination for a period of not less than five years after the filing of the documents based on the information which they contain.

§207. (§437) Time for making reports

(a) Each labor organization shall file the initial report required under section 431(a) of this title within ninety days after the date on which it first becomes subject to this chapter.

(b) Each person required to file a report under section 431(b), 432, 433(a), the second sentence of 433(b), or section 441 of this title shall file such report within ninety days after the end of each of its fiscal years; except that where such person is subject to section 431(b), 432, 433(a), the second sentence of 433(b), or section 441 of this title, as the case may be, for only a portion of such a fiscal year (because September 14, 1959, occurs during such person's fiscal year or such person becomes subject to this chapter during its fiscal year) such person may consider that portion as the entire fiscal year in making such report.

§208. (§438) Rules and regulations; simplified reports

The Secretary shall have authority to issue, amend, and rescind rules and regulations prescribing the form and publication of reports required to be filed under this subchapter and such other reasonable rules and regulations (including rules prescribing reports concerning trusts in which a labor organization is interested) as he may find necessary to prevent the circumvention or evasion of such reporting requirements. In exercising his power under this section the Secretary shall prescribe by general rule simplified reports for labor organizations or employers for whom he finds that by virtue of their size a detailed report would be unduly burdensome, but the Secretary may revoke such provision for simplified forms of any labor organization or employer if he determines, after such investigation as he deems proper and due notice and opportunity for a hearing, that the purposes of this section would be served thereby.

§209. (§439) Violations and penalties

(a) *Willful violations of provisions of subchapter.* Any person who willfully violates this subchapter shall be fined not more than $10,000 or imprisoned for not more than one year, or both.

(b) *False statements or representation of fact with knowledge of falsehood.* Any person who makes a false statement or representation of a material fact, knowing it to be false, or who knowingly fails to disclose a material fact, in any document, report, or other information required under the provisions of this subchapter shall be fined not more than $10,000 or imprisoned for not more than one year, or both.

(c) *False entry in or willful concealment, etc., of books and records.* Any person who willfully makes a false entry in or willfully conceals, withholds, or destroys any books, records, reports, or statements required to be kept by any provision of this subchapter shall be fined not more than $10,000 or imprisoned for not more than one year, or both.

(d) *Personal responsibility of individuals required to sign reports.* Each individual required to sign reports under sections 431 and 433 of this title shall be personally responsible for the filing of such reports and for any statement contained therein which he knows to be false.

§210. (§440) Civil action for enforcement by Secretary; jurisdiction

Whenever it shall appear that any person has violated or is about to violate any of the provisions of this subchapter, the Secretary may bring a civil action for such relief (including injunctions) as may be appropriate. Any such action may be brought in the district court of the United States where the violation occurred or, at the option of the parties, in the United States District Court for the District of Columbia.

§211. (§441) Surety company reports; contents; waiver or modification of requirements respecting contents of reports

Each surety company which issues any bond required by this chapter or the Employee Retirement Income Security Act of 1974 [29 U.S.C. §1001 et seq.] shall file annually with the Secretary, with respect to each fiscal year during which any such bond was in force, a report, in such form and detail as he may prescribe by regulation, filed by the president and treasurer or corresponding principal officers of the surety company, describing its bond experience under each such chapter or Act, including information as to the premiums received, total claims paid, amounts recovered by way of subrogation, administrative and legal expenses and such related data and information as the Secretary shall determine to be necessary in the public interest and to carry out the policy of the chapter. Notwithstanding the foregoing, if the Secretary finds that any such specific information cannot be practicably ascertained or would be uninformative, the Secretary may modify or waive the requirement for such information.

TITLE III. TRUSTEESHIPS

§301. (§461) Reports

(a) *Filing and contents; Annual financial report.* Every labor organization which has or assumes trusteeship over any subordinate labor organization shall file with the Secretary within thirty days after September 14, 1959 or the imposition of any such trusteeship, and semiannually thereafter, a report, signed by its president and treasurer or corresponding principal officers, as well as by the trustees of such subordinate labor organization, containing the following information: (1) the name and address of the subordinate organization; (2) the date of establishing the trusteeship; (3) a detailed statement of the reason or reasons for establishing or continuing the trusteeship; and (4) the nature and extent of participation by the membership of the subordinate organization in the selection of delegates to represent such organization in regular or special conventions or other policy-determining bodies and in the election of officers of the labor organization which has assumed trusteeship over such subordinate organization. The initial report shall also include a full and complete account of the financial condition of such subordinate organization as of the time trusteeship was assumed over it. During the continuance of a trusteeship the labor organization which has assumed trusteeship over a subordinate labor organization shall file on behalf of the subordinate labor organization the annual financial report required by section 431(b) of this title signed by the president and treasurer or corresponding principal officers of the labor organization which has assumed such trusteeship and the trustees of the subordinate labor organization.

(b) *Applicability of other laws.* The provisions of sections 431(c), 435, 436, 438, and 440 of this title shall be applicable to reports filed under this subchapter.

(c) *Penalty for violations.* Any person who willfully violates this section shall be fined not more than $10,000 or imprisoned for not more than one year, or both.

(d) *False statements and entries; failure to disclose material facts, withholding, concealing or destroying documents, books, records, reports, or statements; penalty.* Any person who makes a false statement or representation of a material fact, knowing it to be false, or who knowingly fails to disclose a material fact, in any report required under the provisions of this section or willfully makes any false entry in or willfully withholds, conceals, or destroys any documents, books, records, reports, or statements upon which such report is based, shall be fined not more than $10,000 or imprisoned for not more than one year, or both.

(e) *Personal liability.* Each individual required to sign a report under this section shall be personally responsible for the filing of such report and for any statement contained therein which he knows to be false.

§302. (§462) Purposes for establishment of trusteeship

Trusteeships shall be established and administered by a labor organization over a subordinate body only in accordance with the constitution and bylaws of the organization which has assumed trusteeship over the subordinate body and for the purpose of correcting corruption or financial malpractice, assuring the performance of collective bargaining agreements or other duties of a bargaining representative, restoring democratic procedures, or otherwise carrying out the legitimate objects of such labor organization.

§303. (§463) Unlawful acts relating to labor organization under trusteeship

(a) During any period when a subordinate body of a labor organization is in trusteeship, it shall be unlawful (1) to count the vote of delegates from such body in any convention or election of officers of the labor organization unless the delegates have been chosen by secret ballot in an election in which all the members in good standing of such subordinate body were eligible to participate, or (2) to transfer to such organization any current receipts or other funds of the subordinate body except the normal per capita tax and assessments payable by subordinate bodies not in trusteeship: *Provided,* That nothing herein contained shall prevent the distribution of the assets of a labor organization in accordance with its constitution and bylaws upon the bona fide dissolution thereof.

(b) Any person who willfully violates this section shall be fined not more than $10,000 or imprisoned for not more than one year, or both.

§304. (§464) Civil action for enforcement

(a) *Complaint; investigation; commencement of action by Secretary, member or subordinate body of labor organization; jurisdiction.* Upon the written complaint of any member or subordinate body of a labor organization alleging that such organization has violated the provisions of this subchapter (except section 461 of this title) the Secretary shall investigate the complaint and if the Secretary finds probable cause to believe that such violation has occurred and has not been remedied he shall, without disclosing the identity of the complainant, bring a civil action in any district court of the United States having jurisdiction of the labor organization for such relief (including injunctions) as may be appropriate. Any member of subordinate body of a labor organization affected by any violation of this subchapter (except section 461 of this title) may bring a civil action in any district court of the United States having jurisdiction of the labor organization for such relief (including injunctions) as may be appropriate.

(b) *Venue.* For the purpose of actions under this section, district courts of the United States shall be deemed to have jurisdiction of a labor organization (1) in the district in which the principal office of such labor organization is located, or (2) in any district in which its duly authorized officers or agents are engaged in conducting the affairs of the trusteeship.

(c) *Presumptions of validity or invalidity of trusteeship.* In any proceeding pursuant to this section a trusteeship established by a labor organization in conformity with the procedural requirements of its constitution and bylaws and authorized or ratified after a fair hearing either before the executive board or before such other body as may be provided in accordance with its constitution or bylaws shall be presumed valid for a period of eighteen months from the date of its establishment and shall not be subject to attack during such period except upon clear and convincing proof that the trusteeship was not established or maintained in good faith for a purpose allowable under section 462 of this title. After the expiration of eighteen months the trusteeship shall be presumed invalid in any such proceeding and its discontinuance shall be decreed unless the labor organization shall show by clear and convincing proof that the continuation of the trusteeship is necessary for a purpose allowable under section 462 of this title. In the latter event the court may dismiss the complaint or retain jurisdiction of the cause on such conditions and for such period as it deems appropriate.

§305. (§465) Report to Congress

The Secretary shall submit to the Congress at the expiration of three years from September 14, 1959, a report upon the operation of this subchapter.

§306. (§466) Additional rights and remedies; exclusive jurisdiction of district court; res judicata

The rights and remedies provided by this Subchapter shall be in addition to any and all other rights and remedies at law or in equity: *Provided,* That upon the filing of a complaint by the Secretary the jurisdiction of the district court over such trusteeship shall be exclusive and the final judgment shall be res judicata.

TITLE IV. ELECTIONS

§401. (§481) Terms of office and election procedures

(a) *Officers of national or international labor organizations; manner of election.* Every national or international labor organization, except a federation of national or international labor organization, shall elect its officers not less often than once every five years either by secret ballot among the members in good standing or at a convention of delegates chosen by secret ballot.

(b) *Officers of local labor organizations; manner of election.* Every local labor organization shall elect its officers not less often than once every three years by secret ballot among the members in good standing.

(c) *Requests for distribution of campaign literature; civil action for enforcement; jurisdiction; inspection of membership lists; adequate safeguards to insure fair election.* Every national or international labor organization, except a federation of national or international labor organizations, and every local labor organization, and its officers, shall be under a duty, enforceable at the suit of any bona fide candidate for office in such labor organization in the district court of the United States in which such labor organization maintains its principal office, to comply with all reasonable requests of any candidate to distribute by mail or otherwise at the candidate's expense campaign literature in aid of such person's candidacy to all members in good standing of such labor organization and to refrain from discrimination in favor of or against any candidate with respect to the use of lists of members, and whenever such labor organizations or its officers authorize the distribution by mail or otherwise to members of campaign literature on behalf of any candidate or of the labor organization itself with reference to such election, similar distribution at the request of any other bona fide candidate shall be made by such labor organization and its officers, with equal treatment as to the expense of such distribution. Every bona fide candidate shall have the right, once within 30 days prior to an election of a labor organization in which he is a candidate, to inspect a list containing the names and last known addresses of all members of the labor organization who are subject to a collective bargaining agreement requiring membership therein as a condition of employment, which list shall be maintained and kept at the principal office of such labor organization by a designated official thereof. Adequate safeguards to insure a fair election shall be provided, including the right of any candidate to have an observer at the polls and at the counting of the ballots.

(d) *Officers of intermediate bodies; manner of election.* Officers of intermediate bodies, such as general committees, system boards, joint boards, or joint councils, shall be elected not less often than once every four years by secret ballot among the members in good standing or by labor organization officers representative of such members who have been elected by secret ballot.

(e) *Nomination of candidates; eligibility; notice of election; voting rights; counting and publication of results; preservation of ballots and records.* In any election required by this section which is to be held by secret ballot a reasonable opportunity shall be given for the nomination of candidates and every member in good standing shall be eligible to be a candidate and to hold office (subject to section 504 of this title and to reasonable qualifications uniformly imposed) and shall have the right to vote for or otherwise support the candidate or candidates of his choice, without being subject to penalty, discipline, or improper interference or reprisal of any kind by such organization or any member thereof. Not less than fifteen days prior to the election notice thereof shall be mailed to each member at his last known home address. Each member in good standing shall be entitled to one vote. No member whose dues have been withheld by his employer for payment to such organization pursuant to his voluntary authorization provided for in a collective bargaining agreement shall be declared ineligible to vote or be a candidate for office in such organization by reason of alleged delay or default in the payment of dues. The votes cast by members of each local labor organization shall be counted, and the results published, separately. The election officials designated in the constitution and bylaws or the secretary, if no other official is designated, shall preserve for one year the ballots and other records pertaining to the election. The election shall be conducted in accordance with the constitution and bylaws of such organization insofar as they are not inconsistent with the provisions of this subchapter.

(f) *Election of officers by convention of delegates; manner of conducting convention; preservation of records.* When officers are chosen by a convention of delegates elected by secret ballot, the convention shall be conducted in accordance with the constitution and bylaws of the labor organization insofar as they are not inconsistent with the provisions of this subchapter. The officials designated in the constitution and bylaws or the secretary, if no other is designated, shall preserve for one year the credentials of the delegates and all minutes and other records of the convention pertaining to the election of officers.

(g) *Use of dues, assessments or similar levies, and funds of employer for promotion of candidacy of person.* No moneys received by any labor organization by way of dues, assessment, or similar levy, and no moneys of an employer shall be contributed or applied to promote the candidacy of any person in any election subject to the provisions of this subchapter. Such moneys of a labor organization may be utilized for notices, factual statements of issues not involving candidates, and other expenses necessary for the holding of an election.

(h) *Removal of officers guilty of serious misconduct.* If the Secretary, upon application of any member of a local labor organization, finds after hearing in accordance with subchapter II of chapter 5 of Title 5 that the constitution and bylaws of such labor organization do not provide an adequate procedure for the removal of an elected officer guilty of serious misconduct, such officer may be removed, for cause shown and after notice and hearing, by the members in good standing voting in a secret ballot, conducted by the officers of such labor organization in accordance with its constitution and bylaws insofar as they are not inconsistent with the provisions of this subchapter.

(i) *Rules and regulations for determining adequacy of removal procedures.* The Secretary shall promulgate rules and regulations prescribing minimum standards and procedures for determining the adequacy of the removal procedures to which reference is made in subsection (h) of this section.

§402. (§482) Enforcement

(a) *Filing of complaint; presumption of validity of challenged election.* A member of a labor organization —

(1) who has exhausted the remedies available under the constitution and bylaws of such organization and of any parent body, or

(2) who has invoked such available remedies without obtaining a final decision within three calendar months after their invocation,

may file a complaint with the Secretary within one calendar month thereafter alleging the violation of any provision of section 481 of this title (including violation of the constitution and bylaws of the labor organization pertaining to the election and removal of officers). The challenged election shall be presumed valid pending a final decision thereon (as hereinafter provided) and in the interim the affairs of the organization shall be conducted by the officers elected or in such other manner as its constitution and bylaws may provide.

(b) *Investigation of complaint; commencement of civil action by Secretary; jurisdiction; preservation of assets.* The Secretary shall investigate such complaint and, if he finds probable cause to believe that a violation of this subchapter has occurred and has not been remedied, he shall, within sixty days after the filing of such complaint, bring a civil action against the labor organization as an entity in the district court of the United States in which such labor organization maintains its principal office to set aside the invalid election, if any, and to direct the conduct of an election or hearing and vote upon the removal of officers under the supervision of the Secretary and in accordance with the provisions of this subchapter and such rules and regulations as the Secretary may prescribe. The court shall have power to take such action as it deems proper to preserve the assets of the labor organization.

(c) *Declaration of void election; order for new election; certification of election to court; decree; certification of result of vote for removal of officers.* If, upon a preponderance of the evidence after a trial upon the merits, the court finds —

(1) that an election has not been held within the time prescribed by section 481 of this title, or

(2) that the violation of section 481 of this title may have affected the outcome of an election,

the court shall declare the election, if any, to be void and direct the conduct of a new election under supervision of the Secretary and, so far as lawful and practicable, in conformity with the constitution and bylaws of the labor organization. The Secretary shall promptly certify to the court the names of the persons elected, and the court shall thereupon enter a decree declaring such persons to be the officers of the labor organization. If the proceeding is for the removal of officers pursuant to subsection (h) of section 481 of this title, the Secretary shall certify the results of the vote and the court shall enter a decree declaring whether such persons have been removed as officers of the labor organization.

(d) *Review of orders; stay of order directing election.* An order directing an election, dismissing a complaint, or designating elected officers of a labor organization shall be appealable in the same manner as the final judgment in a civil action, but an order directing an election shall not be stayed pending appeal.

§403. (§483) Application of other laws; existing rights and remedies; exclusiveness of remedy for challenging election

No labor organization shall be required by law to conduct elections of officers with greater frequency or in a different form or manner than is required by its own constitution or bylaws, except as otherwise provided by this subchapter. Existing rights and remedies to enforce the constitution and bylaws of a labor organization with respect to elections prior to the conduct thereof shall not be affected by the provisions of this subchapter. The remedy provided by this subchapter for challenging an election already conducted shall be exclusive.

TITLE V. SAFEGUARDS FOR LABOR ORGANIZATIONS

§501. (§501) Fiduciary responsibility of officers of labor organizations

(a) *Duties of officers; exculpatory provisions and resolutions void.* The officers, agents, shop stewards, and other representatives of a labor organization occupy positions of trust in relation to such organization and its members as a group. It is, therefore, the duty of each such person, taking into account the special problems and functions of a labor organization, to hold its money and property solely for the benefit of the organization and its members and to manage, invest, and expend the same in accordance with its constitution and bylaws and any resolutions of the governing bodies adopted thereunder, to refrain from dealing with such organization as an adverse party or in behalf of an adverse party in any matter connected with his duties and from holding or acquiring any pecuniary or personal interest which conflicts with the interests of such organization, and to account to the organization for any profit received by him in whatever capacity in connection with transactions conducted by him or under his direction on behalf of the organization. A general exculpatory provision in the constitution and bylaws of such a labor organization or a general exculpatory resolution of a governing body purporting to relieve any such person of liability for breach of the duties declared by this section shall be void as against public policy.

(b) *Violation of duties; action by member after refusal or failure by labor organization to commence proceedings; jurisdiction; leave of court; counsel fees and expenses.* When any officer, agent, shop steward, or representative of any labor organization is alleged to have violated the duties declared in subsection (a) of this section and the labor organization or its governing board or officers refuse or fail to sue or recover damages or secure an accounting or other appropriate relief within a reasonable time after being requested to do so by any member of the labor organization, such member may sue such officer, agent, shop steward, or representative in any district court of the United States or in any State court of competent jurisdiction to recover damages or secure an accounting or other appropriate relief for the benefit of the labor organization. No such proceeding shall be brought except upon leave of the court obtained upon verified application and for good cause shown, which application may be made ex parte. The trial judge may allot a reasonable part of the recovery in any action under this subsection to pay the fees of counsel prosecuting the suit at the instance of the member of the labor organization and to compensate such member for any expenses necessarily paid or incurred by him in connection with the litigation.

(c) *Embezzlement of assets; penalty.* Any person who embezzles, steals, or unlawfully and willfully abstracts or converts to his own use, or the use of another, any of the moneys, funds, securities, property, or other assets of a labor organization of which he is an officer, or by which he is employed, directly or indirectly, shall be fined not more than $10,000 or imprisoned for not more than five years, or both.

§502. (§502) Bonding of officers and employees of labor organizations; amount, form, and placement of bonds; penalty for violation

(a) Every officer, agent, shop steward, or other representative or employee of any labor organization (other than a labor organization whose property and annual financial receipts do not exceed $5,000 in value), or of a trust in which a labor organization is interested, who handles funds or other property thereof shall be bonded to provide protection against loss by reason of acts of fraud or dishonesty on his part directly or through connivance with others. The bond of each such person shall be fixed at the beginning of the organization's fiscal year and shall be in an amount not less than 10 per centum of the funds handled by him and his predecessor or predecessors, if any, during the preceding fiscal year, but in no case more than $500,000. If the labor organization or the trust in which a labor organization is interested does not have a preceding fiscal year, the amount of the bond shall be, in the case of a local labor organization, not less than $1,000, and in the case of any other labor organization or of a trust in which a labor organization is interested, not less than $10,000. Such bonds shall be individual or schedule in form, and shall have a corporate surety company as surety thereon. Any person who is not covered by such bonds shall not be permitted to receive, handle, disburse, or otherwise exercise custody or control of the funds or other property of a labor organization or of a trust in which a labor organization is interested. No such bond shall be placed through an agent or broker or with a surety company in which any labor organization or any officer, agent, shop steward, or other representative of a labor organization has any direct or indirect interest. Such surety company shall be a corporate surety which holds a grant of authority from the Secretary of the Treasury under sections 9304-9308 of Title 31, as an acceptable surety on Federal bonds: *Provided,* That when in the opinion of the Secretary a labor organization has made other bonding arrangements which would provide the protection required by this section at comparable cost or less, he may exempt such labor organization from placing a bond through a surety company holding such grant of authority.

(b) Any person who willfully violates this section shall be fined not more than $10,000 or imprisoned for not more than one year, or both.

§504. (§504) Prohibition against certain persons holding office

(a) *Membership in Communist Party; persons convicted of robbery, bribery, etc.* No person who is or has been a member of the Communist Party or who has been convicted of, or served any part of a prison term resulting from his conviction of, robbery, bribery, extortion, embezzlement, grand larceny, burglary, arson, violation of narcotics laws, murder, rape, assault with intent to kill, assault which inflicts grievous bodily injury, or a violation of subchapter III or IV of this chapter, any felony involving abuse or misuse of such person's position or employment in a labor organization or employee benefit plan to seek or obtain an illegal gain at the expense of the members of the labor organization or the beneficiaries of the employee benefit plan, or conspiracy to commit any such crimes or attempt to commit any such crimes, or a crime in which any of the foregoing crimes is an element, shall serve or be permitted to serve —

(1) as a consultant or adviser to any labor organization,

(2) as an officer, director, trustee, member of any executive board or similar governing body, business agent, manager, organizer, employee, or representative in any capacity of any labor organization,

(3) as a labor relations consultant or adviser to a person engaged in an industry or activity affecting commerce, or as an officer, director, agent, or employee of any group or association of employers dealing with any labor organization, or in a position having specific collective bargaining authority or direct responsibility in the area of labor-management relations in any corporation or association engaged in an industry or activity affecting commerce, or

(4) in a position which entitles its occupant to a share of the proceeds of, or as an officer or executive or administrative employee of,

any entity whose activities are in whole or substantial part devoted to providing goods or services to any labor organization, or

(5) in any capacity, other than in his capacity as a member of such labor organization, that involves decisionmaking authority concerning, or decisionmaking authority over, or custody of, or control of the moneys, funds, assets, or property of any labor organization,

during or for the period of thirteen years after such conviction or after the end of such imprisonment, whichever is later, unless the sentencing court on the motion of the person convicted sets a lesser period of at least three years after such conviction or after the end of such imprisonment, whichever is later, or unless prior to the end of such period, in the case of a person so convicted or imprisoned, (A) his citizenship rights, having been revoked as a result of such conviction, have been fully restored, or (B) if the offense is a Federal offense, the sentencing judge or, if the offense is a State or local offense, the United States district court for the district in which the offense was committed, pursuant to sentencing guidelines and policy statements under section 994(a) of Title 28, determines that such person's service in any capacity referred to in clauses (1) through (5) would not be contrary to the purposes of this chapter. Prior to making any such determination the court shall hold a hearing and shall give notice of such proceeding by certified mail to the Secretary of Labor and to State, county, and Federal prosecuting officials in the jurisdiction or jurisdictions in which such person was convicted. The court's determination in any such proceeding shall be final. No person shall knowingly hire, retain, employ, or otherwise place any other person to serve in any capacity in violation of this subsection.

(b) *Penalty for violations.* Any person who willfully violates this section shall be fined not more than $10,000 or imprisoned for not more than five years, or both.

(c) *Definitions.* For the purpose of this section —

(1) A person shall be deemed to have been "convicted" and under the disability of "conviction" from the date of the judgment of the trial court, regardless of whether that judgment remains under appeal.

(2) A period of parole shall not be considered as part of a period of imprisonment.

(d) *Salary of persons barred from labor organization office during appeal of conviction.* Whenever any person —

(1) by operation of this section, has been barred from office or other position in a labor organization as a result of a conviction, and

(2) has filed an appeal of that conviction,

any salary which would be otherwise due such person by virtue of such office or position, shall be placed in escrow by the individual employer or organization responsible for payment of such salary. Payment of such salary into escrow shall continue for the duration of the appeal or for the period of time during which such salary would be otherwise due, whichever period is shorter. Upon the final reversal of such person's conviction on appeal, the amounts in escrow shall be paid to such person. Upon the final sustaining of such person's conviction on appeal, the amounts in escrow shall be returned to the individual employer or organization responsible for payment of those amounts. Upon final reversal of such person's conviction, such person shall no longer be barred by this statute from assuming any position from which such person was previously barred.

TITLE VI. MISCELLANEOUS PROVISIONS

§601. (§521) Investigations by Secretary; applicability of other laws

(a) The Secretary shall have power when he believes it necessary in order to determine whether any person has violated or is about to violate any provision of this chapter (except subchapter II of this chapter) to make an investigation and in connection therewith he may enter such places and inspect such records and accounts and question such persons as he may deem necessary to enable him to determine the facts relative thereto. The Secretary may report to interested persons or officials concerning the facts required to be shown in any report required by this chapter and concerning the reasons for failure or refusal to file such a report or any other matter which he deems to be appropriate as a result of such an investigation.

(b) For the purpose of any investigation provided for in this chapter, the provisions of sections 49 and 50 of title 15 (relating to the attendance of witnesses and the production of books, papers, and documents), are made applicable to the jurisdiction, powers, and duties of the Secretary or any officers designated by him.

§602. (§522) Extortionate picketing; penalty for violation

(a) It shall be unlawful to carry on picketing on or about the premises of any employer for the purpose of, or as part of any conspiracy or in furtherance of any plan or purpose for, the personal profit or enrichment of any individual (except a bona fide increase in wages or other employee benefits) by taking or obtaining any money or other thing of value from such employer against his will or with his consent.

(b) Any person who willfully violates this section shall be fined not more than $10,000 or imprisoned not more than twenty years, or both.

§603. (§523) Retention of rights under other Federal and State laws

(a) Except as explicitly provided to the contrary, nothing in this chapter shall reduce or limit the responsibilities of any labor organization or any officer, agent, shop steward, or other representative of a labor organization, or of any trust in which a labor organization is interested, under any other Federal law or under the laws of any State, and, except as explicitly provided to the contrary, nothing in this chapter shall take away any right or bar any remedy to which members of a labor organization are entitled under such other Federal law or law of any State.

(b) Nothing contained in this chapter and section 186(a)-(c) of this title shall be construed to supersede or impair or otherwise affect the provisions of the Railway Labor Act, as amended [45 U.S.C. §151 et seq.], or any of the obligations, rights, benefits, privileges, or immunities of any carrier, employee, organization, representative, or person subject thereto; nor shall anything contained in this chapter be construed to confer any rights, privileges, immunities, or defenses upon employers, or to impair or otherwise affect the rights of any person under the National Labor Relations Act, as amended [29 U.S.C. §151 et seq.].

§604. (§524) Effect on State laws

Nothing in this chapter shall be construed to impair or diminish the authority of any State to enact and enforce general criminal laws with respect to robbery, bribery, extortion, embezzlement, grand larceny, burglary, arson, violation of narcotics laws, murder, rape, assault with intent to kill, or assault which inflicts grievous bodily injury, or conspiracy to commit any of such crimes.

§2201. (§524a) Elimination of racketeering activities threat; State legislation governing collective bargaining representative*

Notwithstanding this or any other Act regulating labor-management relations, each State shall have the authority to enact and enforce, as part of a comprehensive statutory system to eliminate the threat of pervasive racketeering activity in an industry that is, or over time has been, affected by such activity, a provision of law that applies equally to employers, employees, and collective bargaining representatives, which provision of law governs service in any position in a local labor organization which acts or seeks to act in that State as a collective bargaining representative pursuant to the National Labor Relations Act [29 U.S.C. §151 et seq.], in the industry that is subject to that program.

§605. (§525) Service of process

For the purposes of this chapter, service of summons, subpena, or other legal process of a court of the United States upon an officer or agent of a labor organization in his capacity as such shall constitute service upon the labor organization.

§606. (§526) Applicability of administrative procedure provisions

The provisions of subchapter II of chapter 5, and chapter 7, of title 5 shall be applicable to the issuance, amendment, or rescission of any rules or regulations, or any adjudication authorized or required pursuant to the provisions of this chapter.

§607. (§527) Cooperation with other agencies and departments

In order to avoid unnecessary expense and duplication of functions among Government agencies, the Secretary may make such arrangements or agreements for cooperation or mutual assistance in the performance of his functions under this chapter and the functions of any such agency as he may find to be practicable and consistent with law. The Secretary may utilize the facilities or services of any department,

---

*This section was added by Pub. L. 98-473, Title II, §2201, Oct. 12, 1984, 98 Stat. 2192.

agency, or establishment of the United States or of any State or political subdivision of a State, including the services of any of its employees, with the lawful consent of such department, agency, or establishment; and each department, agency, or establishment of the United States is authorized and directed to cooperate with the Secretary and, to the extent permitted by law, to provide such information and facilities as he may request for his assistance in the performance of his functions under this chapter. The Attorney General or his representative shall receive from the Secretary for appropriate action such evidence developed in the performance of his functions under this chapter as may be found to warrant consideration for criminal prosecution under the provisions of this chapter or other Federal law.

§608. (§528) Criminal contempt

No person shall be punished for any criminal contempt allegedly committed outside the immediate presence of the court in connection with any civil action prosecuted by the Secretary or any other person in any court of the United States under the provisions of this chapter unless the facts constituting such criminal contempt are established by the verdict of the jury in a proceeding in the district court of the United States, which jury shall be chosen and empaneled in the manner prescribed by the law governing trial juries in criminal prosecutions in the district courts of the United States.

§609. (§529) Prohibition on certain discipline by labor organization

It shall be unlawful for any labor organization, or any officer, agent, shop steward, or other representative of a labor organization, or any employee thereof to fine, suspend, expel, or otherwise discipline any of its members for exercising any right to which he is entitled under the provisions of this chapter. The provisions of section 412 of this title shall be applicable in the enforcement of this section.

§610. (§530) Deprivation of rights by violence; penalty

It shall be unlawful for any person through the use of force or violence, or threat of the use of force or violence, to restrain, coerce, or intimidate, or attempt to restrain, coerce, or intimidate any member of a labor organization for the purpose of interfering with or preventing the exercise of any right to which he is entitled under the provisions of this chapter. Any person who willfully violates this section shall be fined not more than $1,000 or imprisoned for not more than one year, or both.

§611. (§531) Separability of provisions

If any provision of this chapter, or the application of such provision to any person or circumstances, shall be held invalid, the remainder of this chapter or the application of such provision to persons or circumstances other than those as to which it is held invalid, shall not be affected thereby.

Federal Arbitration Act — Selected Provisions
61 Stat. 669 (1947), as amended, 9 U.S.C. §§1 et seq.[*]

§1. "Maritime transactions" and "commerce" defined; exceptions to operation of title

"Maritime transactions", as herein defined, means charter parties, bills of lading of water carriers, agreements relating to wharfage, supplies furnished vessels or repairs to vessels, collisions, or any other matters in foreign commerce which, if the subject of controversy, would be embraced within admiralty jurisdiction; "commerce", as herein defined, means commerce among the several States or with foreign nations, or in any Territory of the United States or in the District of Columbia, or between any such Territory and another, or between any such Territory and any State or foreign nation, or between the District of Columbia and any State or Territory or foreign nation, but nothing herein contained shall apply to contracts of employment of seamen, railroad employees, or any other class of workers engaged in foreign or interstate commerce.

§2. Validity, irrevocability and enforcement of agreements to arbitrate

A written provision in any maritime transaction or a contract evidencing a transaction involving commerce to settle by arbitration a controversy thereafter arising out of such contract or transaction, or the refusal to perform the whole or any part thereof, or an agreement in writing to submit to arbitration an existing controversy arising out of such a contract, transaction, or refusal, shall be valid, irrevocable, and enforceable, save upon such grounds as exist at law or in equity for the revocation of any contract.

§3. Stay of proceedings where issue therein referable to arbitration

If any suit or proceeding be brought in any of the courts of the United States upon any issue referable to arbitration under an agreement in writing for such arbitration, the court in which such suit is pending, upon being satisfied that the issue involved in such suit or proceeding is referable to arbitration under such an agreement, shall on application of

---

[*]This law is derived from Act of Feb. 12, 1925, c.213, 43 Stat. 883.—EDS.

one of the parties stay the trial of the action until such arbitration has been had in accordance with the terms of the agreement, providing the applicant for the stay is not in default in proceeding with such arbitration.

§4. Failure to arbitrate under agreement; petition to United States court having jurisdiction for order to compel arbitration; notice and service thereof; hearing and determination

A party aggrieved by the alleged failure, neglect, or refusal of another to arbitrate under a written agreement for arbitration may petition any United States district court which, save for such agreement, would have jurisdiction under Title 28, in a civil action or in admiralty of the subject matter of a suit arising out of the controversy between the parties, for an order directing that such arbitration proceed in the manner provided for in such agreement. . . .

§5. Appointment of arbitrators or umpire

If in the agreement provision be made for a method of naming or appointing an arbitrator or arbitrators or an umpire, such method shall be followed; but if no method be provided therein, or if a method be provided and any party thereto shall fail to avail himself of such method, or if for any other reason there shall be a lapse in the naming of an arbitrator or arbitrators or umpire, or in filling a vacancy, then upon the application of either party to the controversy the court shall designate and appoint an arbitrator or arbitrators or umpire, as the case may require, who shall act under the said agreement with the same force and effect as if he or they had been specifically named therein; and unless otherwise provided in the agreement the arbitration shall be by a single arbitrator.

§9. Award of arbitrators; confirmation; jurisdiction; procedure

If the parties in their agreement have agreed that a judgment of the court shall be entered upon the award made pursuant to the arbitration, and shall specify the court, then at any time within one year after the award is made any party to the arbitration may apply to the court so specified for an order confirming the award, and thereupon the court must grant such an order unless the award is vacated, modified, or corrected as prescribed in sections 10 and 11 of this title. If no court is specified in the agreement of the parties, then such application may be made to the United States court in and for the district within which such award was made. . . .

§10. Same; vacation; grounds; rehearing

(a) In any of the following cases the United States court in and for the district wherein the award was made may make an order vacating the award upon the application of any party to the arbitration —

(1) where the award was procured by corruption, fraud, or undue means;

(2) where there was evident partiality or corruption in the arbitrators, or either of them;

(3) where the arbitrators were guilty of misconduct in refusing to postpone the hearing, upon sufficient cause shown, or in refusing to hear evidence pertinent and material to the controversy; or of any other misbehavior by which the rights of any party have been prejudiced; or

(4) where the arbitrators exceeded their powers, or so imperfectly executed them that a mutual, final, and definite award upon the subject matter submitted was not made.

(b) If an award is vacated and the time within which the agreement required the award to be made has not expired, the court may, in its discretion, direct a rehearing by the arbitrators.

(c) The United States district court for the district wherein an award was made that was issued pursuant to section 580 of title 5 may make an order vacating the award upon the application of a person, other than a party to the arbitration, who is adversely affected or aggrieved by the award, if the use of arbitration or the award is clearly inconsistent with the factors set forth in section 572 of title 5.[*]

§11. Same; modification or correction; grounds; order

In either of the following cases the United States court in and for the district wherein the award was made may make an order modifying

---

[*]As added by Pub. L. 101-552 (1990) and redesignated as subsection "c" by Pub. L. 107-169 (2002).

or correcting the award upon the application of any party to the arbitration —

(a) Where there was an evident material miscalculation of figures or an evident material mistake in the description of any person, thing, or property referred to in the award.

(b) Where the arbitrators have awarded upon a matter not submitted to them, unless it is a matter not affecting the merits of the decision upon the matter submitted.

(c) Where the award is imperfect in matter of form not affecting the merits of the controversy.

The order may modify and correct the award, so as to effect the intent thereof and promote justice between the parties.

§12. Notice of motions to vacate or modify; service; stay of proceedings

Notice of a motion to vacate, modify, or correct an award must be served upon the adverse party or his attorney within three months after the award is filed or delivered. . . . For the purposes of the motion any judge who might make an order to stay the proceedings in an action brought in the same court may make an order, to be served with the notice of motion, staying the proceedings of the adverse party to enforce the award.

United States Bankruptcy Code — Selected Provisions[*]
92 Stat. 2549 (1978), as amended, 11 U.S.C. §§101 et seq.

§1113. Rejection of collective bargaining agreements[**]

(a) The debtor in possession, or the trustee if one has been appointed under the provisions of this chapter, other than a trustee in a case covered by subchapter IV of this chapter and by title I of the Railway Labor Act, may assume or reject a collective bargaining agreement only in accordance with the provisions of this section.

(b)(1) Subsequent to filing a petition and prior to filing an application seeking rejection of a collective bargaining agreement, the debtor in possession or trustee (hereinafter in this section, "trustee" shall include a debtor in possession), shall —

(A) make a proposal to the authorized representative of the employees covered by such agreement, based on the most complete and reliable information available at the time of such proposal, which provides for those necessary modifications in the employees benefits and protections that are necessary to permit the reorganization of the debtor and assures that all creditors, the debtor and all of the affected parties are treated fairly and equitably; and

(B) provide, subject to subsection (d)(3), the representative of the employees with such relevant information as is necessary to evaluate the proposal.

(2) During the period beginning on the date of the making of a proposal provided for in paragraph (1) and ending on the date of the hearing provided for in subsection (d)(1), the trustee shall meet, at reasonable times, with the authorized representative to confer in good faith in attempting to reach mutually satisfactory modifications of such agreement.

(c) The court shall approve an application for rejection of a collective bargaining agreement only if the court finds that —

(1) the trustee has, prior to the hearing, made a proposal that fulfills the requirements of subsection (b)(1);

(2) the authorized representative of the employees has refused to accept such proposal without good cause; and

(3) the balance of the equities clearly favors rejection of such agreement.

---

[*]Section references are to the United States Code.—EDS.
[**]Added by Pub. L. 98-353, Title III, §541(a), July 10, 1984, 98 Stat. 390.

(d)(1) Upon the filing of an application for rejection the court shall schedule a hearing to be held not later than fourteen days after the date of the filing of such application. All interested parties may appear and be heard at such hearing. Adequate notice shall be provided to such parties at least ten days before the date of such hearing. The court may extend the time for the commencement of such hearing for a period not exceeding seven days where the circumstances of the case, and the interests of justice require such extension, or for additional periods of time to which the trustee and representative agree.

(2) The court shall rule on such application for rejection within thirty days after the date of the commencement of the hearing. In the interests of justice, the court may extend such time for ruling for such additional period as the trustee and the employees' representative may agree to. If the court does not rule on such application within thirty days after the date of the commencement of the hearing, or within such additional time as the trustee and the employees' representative may agree to, the trustee may terminate or alter any provisions of the collective bargaining agreement pending the ruling of the court on such application.

(3) The court may enter such protective orders, consistent with the need of the authorized representative of the employee (sic) to evaluate the trustee's proposal and the application for rejection, as may be necessary to prevent disclosure of information provided to such representative where such disclosure could compromise the position of the debtor with respect to its competitors in the industry in which it is engaged.

(e) If during a period when the collective bargaining agreement continues in effect, and if essential to the continuation of the debtor's business, or in order to avoid irreparable damage to the estate, the court, after notice and a hearing, may authorize the trustee to implement interim changes in the terms, conditions, wages, benefits, or work rules provided by a collective bargaining agreement. Any hearing under this paragraph shall be scheduled in accordance with the needs of the trustee. The implementation of such interim changes shall not render the application for rejection moot.

(f) No provision of this title shall be construed to permit a trustee to unilaterally terminate or alter any provisions of a collective bargaining agreement prior to compliance with the provisions of this section.

§1114. Payment of insurance benefits to retired employees

(a) For purposes of this section, the term "retiree benefits" means payments to any entity or person for the purpose of providing or reimbursing payments for retired employees and their spouses and dependents, for medical, surgical, or hospital care benefits, or benefits in the event of sickness, accident, disability, or death under any plan, fund, or program (through the purchase of insurance or otherwise) maintained or established in whole or in part by the debtor prior to filing a petition commencing a case under this title.

(b)(1) For purposes of this section, the term "authorized representative" means the authorized representative designated pursuant to subsection (c) for persons receiving any retiree benefits covered by a collective bargaining agreement or subsection (d) in the case of persons receiving retiree benefits not covered by such an agreement.

(2) Committees of retired employees appointed by the court pursuant to this section shall have the same rights, powers, and duties as committees appointed under sections 1102 and 1103 of this title for the purpose of carrying out the purposes of sections 1114 and 1129(a)(13) and, as permitted by the court, shall have the power to enforce the rights of persons under this title as they relate to retiree benefits.

(c)(1) A labor organization shall be, for purposes of this section, the authorized representative of those persons receiving any retiree benefits covered by any collective bargaining agreement to which that labor organization is signatory, unless (A) such labor organization elects not to serve as the authorized representative of such persons, or (B) the court, upon a motion by any party in interest, after notice and hearing, determines that different representation of such persons is appropriate.

(2) In cases where the labor organization referred to in paragraph (1) elects not to serve as the authorized representative of those persons receiving any retiree benefits covered by any collective bargaining agreement to which that labor organization is signatory, or in cases where the court, pursuant to paragraph (1) finds different representation of such persons appropriate, the court, upon a motion by any party in interest, and after notice and a hearing, shall appoint a committee of retired employees if the debtor seeks to modify or not pay the retiree benefits or if the court otherwise determines that it is appropriate, from among such persons, to serve as the authorized representative of such persons under this section.

(d) The court, upon a motion by any party in interest, and after notice and a hearing, shall appoint a committee of retired employees if the debtor seeks to modify or not pay the retiree benefits or if the court otherwise determines that it is appropriate, to serve as the authorized representative, under this section, of those persons receiving any retiree benefits not covered by a collective bargaining agreement.

(e)(1) Notwithstanding any other provision of this title, the debtor in possession, or the trustee if one has been appointed under the provisions of this chapter (hereinafter in this section "trustee" shall include a debtor in possession), shall timely pay and shall not modify any retiree benefits, except that —

 (A) the court, on motion of the trustee or authorized representative, and after notice and a hearing, may order modification of such payments, pursuant to the provisions of subsections (g) and (h) of this section, or

 (B) the trustee and the authorized representative of the recipients of those benefits may agree to modification of such payments, after which such benefits as modified shall continue to be paid by the trustee.

(2) Any payment for retiree benefits required to be made before a plan confirmed under section 1129 of this title is effective has the status of an allowed administrative expense as provided in section 503 of this title.

(f)(1) Subsequent to filing a petition and prior to filing an application seeking modification of the retiree benefits, the trustee shall —

 (A) make a proposal to the authorized representative of the retirees, based on the most complete and reliable information available at the time of such proposal, which provides for those necessary modifications in the retiree benefits that are necessary to permit the reorganization of the debtor and assures that all creditors, the debtor and all of the affected parties are treated fairly and equitably; and

 (B) provide, subject to subsection (k)(3), the representative of the retirees with such relevant information as is necessary to evaluate the proposal.

(2) During the period beginning on the date of the making of a proposal provided for in paragraph (1), and ending on the date of the hearing provided for in subsection (k)(1), the trustee shall meet, at reasonable times, with the authorized representative to confer in good faith in attempting to reach mutually satisfactory modifications of such retiree benefits.

(g) The court shall enter an order providing for modification in the payment of retiree benefits if the court finds that —

(1) the trustee has, prior to the hearing, made a proposal that fulfills the requirements of subsection (f);

(2) the authorized representative of the retirees has refused to accept such proposal without good cause; and

(3) such modification is necessary to permit the reorganization of the debtor and assures that all creditors, the debtor, and all of the affected parties are treated fairly and equitably, and is clearly favored by the balance of the equities;

except that in no case shall the court enter an order providing for such modification which provides for a modification to a level lower than that proposed by the trustee in the proposal found by the court to have complied with the requirements of this subsection and subsection (f): *Provided, however,* That at any time after an order is entered providing for modification in the payment of retiree benefits, or at any time after an agreement modifying such benefits is made between the trustee and the authorized representative of the recipients of such benefits, the authorized representative may apply to the court for an order increasing those benefits which order shall be granted if the increase in retiree benefits sought is consistent with the standard set forth in paragraph (3): *Provided further,* That neither the trustee nor the authorized representative is precluded from making more than one motion for a modification order governed by this subsection.

(h)(1) Prior to a court issuing a final order under subsection (g) of this section, if essential to the continuation of the debtor's business, or in order to avoid irreparable damage to the estate, the court, after notice and a hearing, may authorize the trustee to implement interim modifications in retiree benefits.

(2) Any hearing under this subsection shall be scheduled in accordance with the needs of the trustee.

(3) The implementation of such interim changes does not render the motion for modification moot.

(i) No retiree benefits paid between the filing of the petition and the time a plan confirmed under section 1129 of this title becomes effective shall be deducted or offset from the amounts allowed as claims for any benefits which remain unpaid, or from the amounts to be paid under the plan with respect to such claims for unpaid benefits, whether such claims for unpaid benefits are based upon or arise from a right to future unpaid benefits or from any benefits not paid as a result of modifications allowed pursuant to this section.

(j) No claim for retiree benefits shall be limited by section 502(b)(7) of this title.

(k)(1) Upon the filing of an application for modifying retiree benefits, the court shall schedule a hearing to be held not later than fourteen days after the date of the filing of such application. All interested parties may appear and be heard at such hearing. Adequate notice shall be provided to such parties at least ten days before the date of such hearing. The court may extend the time for the commencement of such hearing for a period not exceeding seven days where the circumstances of the case, and the interests of justice require such extension, or for additional periods of time to which the trustee and the authorized representative agree.

(2) The court shall rule on such application for modification within ninety days after the date of the commencement of the hearing. In the interests of justice, the court may extend such time for ruling for such additional period as the trustee and the authorized representative may agree to. If the court does not rule on such application within ninety days after the date of the commencement of the hearing, or within such additional time as the trustee and the authorized representative may agree to, the trustee may implement the proposed modifications pending the ruling of the court on such application.

(3) The court may enter such protective orders, consistent with the need of the authorized representative of the retirees to evaluate the trustee's proposal and the application for modification, as may be necessary to prevent disclosure of information provided to such representative where such disclosure could compromise the position of the debtor with respect to its competitors in the industry in which it is engaged.

(*l*) This section shall not apply to any retiree, or the spouse or dependents of such retiree, if such retiree's gross income for the twelve months preceding the filing of the bankruptcy petition equals or exceeds $250,000, unless such retiree can demonstrate to the satisfaction of the court that he is unable to obtain health, medical, life, and disability coverage for himself, his spouse, and his dependents who would otherwise be covered by the employer's insurance plan, comparable to the coverage provided by the employer on the day before the filing of a petition under this title.

§1167. Collective bargaining agreements

Notwithstanding section 365 of this title, neither the court nor the trustee may change the wages or working conditions of employees of the debtor established by a collective bargaining agreement that is subject to the Railway Labor Act except in accordance with section 6 of such Act.

Selected Forms

National Labor Relations Board

Form NLRB-501   Charge Against Employer
Form NLRB-502   Petition
Form NLRB-508   Charge Against Labor Organization or Its Agents

National Mediation Board

Form NMB-1   Application for Investigation of Representation Dispute
Form NMB-2   Application for Mediation Services

FORM NLRB-501
(11-94)

UNITED STATES OF AMERICA
NATIONAL LABOR RELATIONS BOARD
CHARGE AGAINST EMPLOYER

FORM EXEMPT UNDER 44 U.S.C. 3512

DO NOT WRITE IN THIS SPACE	
Case	Date Filed

INSTRUCTIONS:
File an original and 4 copies of this charge with NLRB Regional Director for the region in which the alleged unfair labor practice occurred or is occurring.

1. EMPLOYER AGAINST WHOM CHARGE IS BROUGHT		
a. Name of Employer		b. Number of Workers Employed
c. Address *(street, city, State, ZIP, Code)*	d. Employer Representative	e. Telephone No.
		Fax No.
f. Type of Establishment *(factory, mine, wholesaler, etc.)*	g. Identify Principal Product or Service	

h. The above-named employer has engaged in and is engaging in unfair labor practices within the meaning of Section 8(a), subsections (1) and *(list subsections)* _____ of the National Labor Relations Act, and these unfair labor practices are unfair practices affecting commerce within the meaning of the Act.

2. Basis of the Charge *(set forth a clear and concise statement of the facts constituting the alleged unfair labor practices.)*

By the above and other acts, the above-named employer has interfered with, restrained, and coerced employees in the exercise of the rights guaranteed in Section 7 of the Act.

3. Full name of party filing charge *(if labor organization, give full name, including local name and number)*

4a. Address *(street and number, city, State, and ZIP Code)*	4b. Telephone No.
	Fax No.

5. Full name of national or international labor organization of which it is an affiliate or constituent unit *(to be filled in when charge is filed by a labor organization)*

6. DECLARATION
I declare that I have read the above charge and that the statements are true to the best of my knowledge and belief.

By _____   _____
    (Signature of representative or person making charge)   *(Title, if any)*

                                                    Fax No. _____

Address _____   _____
                                                    (Telephone No.)   Date

WILLFUL FALSE STATEMENTS ON THIS CHARGE CAN BE PUNISHED BY FINE AND IMPRISONMENT (U.S. CODE, TITLE 18, SECTION 1001)

FORM NLRB-502
(3-96)

FORM EXEMPT UNDER 44 U.S.C. 3512

UNITED STATES GOVERNMENT
NATIONAL LABOR RELATIONS BOARD
PETITION

DO NOT WRITE IN THIS SPACE	
Case No.	Date Filed

INSTRUCTIONS: Submit an original and 4 copies of this Petition to the NLRB Regional Office in the Region in which the employer concerned is located. If more space is required for any one item, attach additional sheets, numbering item accordingly.

The Petitioner alleges that the following circumstances exist and requests that the National Labor Relations Board proceed under its proper authority pursuant to Section 9 of the National Labor Relations Act.

1. **PURPOSE OF THIS PETITION** *(If box RC, RM, or RD is checked and a charge under Section 8(b)(7) of the Act has been filed involving the Employer named herein, the statement following the description of the type of petition shall not be deemed made.)* **(Check One)**

☐ **RC-CERTIFICATION OF REPRESENTATIVE** - A substantial number of employees wish to be represented for purposes of collective bargaining by Petitioner and Petitioner desires to be certified as representative of the employees.

☐ **RM-REPRESENTATION (EMPLOYER PETITION)** - One or more individuals or labor organizations have presented a claim to Petitioner to be recognized as the representative of employees of Petitioner.

☐ **RD-DECERTIFICATION (REMOVAL OF REPRESENTATIVE)** - A substantial number of employees assert that the certified or currently recognized bargaining representative is no longer their representative.

☐ **UD-WITHDRAWAL OF UNION SHOP AUTHORITY (REMOVAL OF OBLIGATION TO PAY DUES)** - Thirty percent (30%) or more of employees in a bargaining unit covered by an agreement between their employer and a labor organization desire that such authority be rescinded.

☐ **UC-UNIT CLARIFICATION** - A labor organization is currently recognized by Employer, but Petitioner seeks clarification of placement of certain employees: *(Check one)* ☐ In unit not previously certified. ☐ In unit previously certified in Case No. _____

☐ **AC-AMENDMENT OF CERTIFICATION** - Petitioner seeks amendment of certification issued in Case No. _____ *Attach statement describing the specific amendment sought.*

2. Name of Employer	Employer Representative to contact	Telephone Number
3. Address(es) of Establishment(s) involved *(Street and number, city, State, ZIP code)*		Telecopier Number (Fax)

4a. Type of Establishment *(Factory, mine, wholesaler, etc.)*	4b. Identify principal product or service

5. Unit involved *(in UC petition, describe present bargaining unit and attached description of proposed clarification.)*	6a. Number of Employees in Unit:
Included	Present
	Proposed *(By UC/AC)*
Excluded	6b. Is this petition supported by 30% or more of the employees in the unit?* ☐ Yes ☐ No
(If you have checked box RC in 1 above, check and complete EITHER item 7a or 7b, whichever is applicable.)	*Not applicable in RM, UC, and AC

7a. ☐ Request for recognition as Bargaining Representative was made on *(Date)* _____ and Employer declined recognition on or about *(Date)* _____ *(If no reply received, so state.)*

7b. ☐ Petitioner is currently recognized as Bargaining Representative and desires certification under the Act.

8. Name of Recognized or Certified Bargaining Agent *(If none, so state.)*	Affiliation
Address, Telephone No. and Telecopier No. (Fax)	Date of Recognition or Certification

9. Expiration Date of Current Contract, If any *(Month, Day, Year)*	10. If you have checked box UD in 1 above, show here the date of execution of agreement granting union shop *(Month, Day, and Year)*

11a. Is there now a strike or picketing at the Employer's establishment(s) involved? Yes _____ No _____	11b. If so, approximately how many employees are participating?

11c. The Employer has been picketed by or on behalf of *(Insert Name)* _____, a labor organization, of *(Insert Address)* _____ Since *(Month, Day, Year)* _____

12. Organizations or individuals other than Petitioner *(and other than those named in Items 8 and 11c)*, which have claimed recognition as representatives and other organizations and individuals known to have a representative interest in any employees in unit described in item 5 above. *(If none, so state.)*

Name	Affiliation	Address	Date of Claim
			Telecopier No. (Fax)

13. Full name of party filing petition *(If labor organization, give full name, including local name and number)*

14a. Address *(street and number, city, state, and ZIP code)*	14b. Telephone No.
	14c. Telecopier No. (Fax)

15. Full name of national or international labor organization of which it is an affiliate or constituent unit *(to be filled in when petition is filed by a labor organization)*

I declare that I have read the above petition and that the statements are true to the best of my knowledge and belief.

Name *(Print)*	Signature	Title *(if any)*
Address *(street and number, city, state, and ZIP code)*		Telephone No.
		Telecopier No. (Fax)

WILLFUL FALSE STATEMENTS ON THIS PETITION CAN BE PUNISHED BY FINE AND IMPRISONMENT (U.S. CODE, TITLE 18, SECTION 1001)

FORM NLRB-508
(6-90)

FORM EXEMPT UNDER 44 U.S.C. 3512

UNITED STATES OF AMERICA
NATIONAL LABOR RELATIONS BOARD
**CHARGE AGAINST LABOR ORGANIZATION
OR ITS AGENTS**

DO NOT WRITE IN THIS SPACE	
Case	Date Filed

INSTRUCTIONS: File an original and 4 copies of this charge and an additional copy for each organization, each local, and each individual named in item 1 with the NLRB Regional Director of the region in which the alleged unfair labor practice occurred or is occurring.

1. LABOR ORGANIZATION OR ITS AGENTS AGAINST WHICH CHARGE IS BROUGHT

a. Name	b. Union Representative to contact

c. Telephone No.	d. Address (street, city, state and ZIP code)

e. The above-named organization(s) or its agents has *(have)* engaged in and is *(are)* engaging in unfair labor practices within the meaning of section 8(b), subsection(s) *(list subsections)* _____ of the National Labor Relations Act, and these unfair labor practices are unfair practices affecting commerce within the meaning of the Act.

2. Basis of the Charge *(set forth a clear and concise statement of the facts constituting the alleged unfair labor practices)*

3. Name of Employer	4. Telephone No.

5. Location of plant involved (street, city, state and ZIP code)	6. Employer representative to contact

7. Type of establishment (factory, mine, wholesaler, etc.)	8. Identify principal product or service	9. Number of workers employed

10. Full name of party filing charge

11. Address of party filing charge (street, city, state and ZIP code)	12. Telephone No.

13. DECLARATION

I declare that I have read the above charge and that the statements therein are true to the best of my knowledge and belief.

By _____
(signature of representative or person making charge)   *(title or office, if any)*

Address _____
                        (Telephone No.)   *(date)*

WILLFUL FALSE STATEMENTS ON THIS CHARGE CAN BE PUNISHED BY FINE AND IMPRISONMENT (U. S. CODE, TITLE 18, SECTION 1001)

*U.S. GPO: 2000-464-640/29074

Form NMB - 1 OMB No. 3140-0001 (Expiration Date 10/31/2005)

Application for Investigation of Representation Dispute

Date: _____

TO THE NATIONAL MEDIATION BOARD, Washington, D. C. 20572: A dispute has arisen among the employees of:

Name of Carrier:		Address:	
Contact:		City, State, Zip Code:	
Telephone Number:		Fax Number:	

as to who is the representative of these employees designated and authorized in accordance with the requirements of the Railway Labor Act. The undersigned, one of the parties to the dispute, hereby requests the National Mediation Board to investigate this dispute, and to certify the name or names of the individuals or organizations authorized to represent the employees involved in accordances with section 2, Ninth, of the Act.

PARTIES TO DISPUTE

Petitioning organization or representative:		
Organization holding existing agreement, if any:	Date:	
Other organization or representatives involved in dispute:		

CRAFT OR CLASS of Employees Involved – (If more than one craft or class, list separately)

	Craft or Class	Number of Employees
1.		
2.		
3.		
4.		
5.		
6.		

EVIDENCE OF REPRESENTATION – this application is supported by (check applicable box):

	At least a majority, if the employees are represented and there is a valid collective bargaining agreement.
	At least 35%, if the employees are unrepresented.

Name and Signature:			
Title:			
Address:		Telephone:	
City, State, Zip Code:		Fax:	

Instructions: Continue to page 2.*   **Form Number Replaced:** This form was previously NMB-3.
Revised October 31, 2002

---

*[Page 2, Applicant Notice of Appearance, deleted.—EDS.]

Form NMB-2 OMB No. 3140-0002 (Expiration Date 9/30/2005)

Application for Mediation Services

TO THE NATIONAL MEDIATION BOARD, Washington, D. C. 20572: A dispute has arisen between the parties shown below which has not been adjusted between them, and the services of the National Mediation Board under Section 5, First, of the Railway Labor Act, are hereby invoked on specific questions set forth below. The approximate number of employees involved is _____ in the craft(s) or class(es) of

_____ .

THE SPECIFIC ISSUE(S) IN DISPUTE (If necessary extend question on additional sheet or attach exhibit):

PARTIES TO DISPUTE

	Carrier		Organization/Individual
Carrier Name		Organization Name	
L. R. Official/Title		Organization Official/Title	
Address		Address	
City, State and Zip Code		City, State and Zip Code	
Telephone		Telephone	
Fax		Fax	
Email		Email	

WORKING AGREEMENT

If an agreement governing rates of pay, rules, or working conditions is in effect, give name of parties thereto and date thereof. If there is no such agreement, so state _____ .

COMPLIANCE WITH RAILWAY LABOR ACT

1. If this dispute involves change in the above-mentioned agreement, attach copy of the 30-day notice served by party desiring change and insert date of notice here _____ .

2. If this dispute involves the negotiation of a new or supplemental agreement, attach copy of request made by party desiring same and insert date of request here _____ .

3. If there has been refusal to confer, so state and give reason; otherwise, give date of last conference here _____ .

Signed at _____ this _____ of _____ 20_____ .
　　　　　　　　　　　　　　(City and State)　　　　　　　　　　　　　　　(Day)　　　　　　(Month)

	Carrier Official	Organization Official
Name:		
Title:		
Signature:		

Filing Instructions: File this application in duplicate.　　　　**Additional Sheets:** Use and attach additional sheets as needed.

According to the Paperwork Reduction Act of 1995, no persons are required to respond to a collection of information unless it displays a valid OMB control Number. The valid OMB control number for this information collection is 3140-0002. The time required to complete this information collection is estimated to average 15 minutes per response, including the time to review instructions, search existing data resources, gather the data needed, and complete and review the information collection.

Revised September 30, 2002

Selected Agreements

2000-2003 National Agreement Between General Electric Company and the International Union of Electronic, Electrical, Salaried, Machine and Furniture Workers (AFL-CIO) and its Affiliated GE-IUE (AFL-CIO) Locals — Selected Provisions

ARTICLE I. UNION RECOGNITION

1. The Company agrees to recognize the Union on behalf of and in conjunction with its Locals for those bargaining units of Company employees for which the Union or any of its Locals, through National Labor Relations Board certifications, is designated as the exclusive collective bargaining representative of employees within such units for the purpose of collective bargaining in respect to rates of pay, wages, hours of employment and other conditions of employment.

2. Where the Union or any of its Locals through National Labor Relations Board certifications shall have been lawfully designated as the exclusive collective bargaining representative for any additional bargaining units of Company employees, such certified representative shall be recognized as provided above and become a party hereto, and the terms of this National Agreement shall thereupon be applicable to the employees within such unit.

ARTICLE II. UNION SECURITY

1. *Agency Shop*

(a) Subject to applicable law, all employees who, as of the date of this Agreement are members of the Union in good standing in accordance with the constitution and bylaws of the Union or who become members of the Union following the effective date of this Agreement, shall, as a condition of employment, remain members of the Union in good standing insofar as the payment of an amount equal to the periodic dues and initiation fees, uniformly required, is concerned.

(b) Subject to applicable law, all present employees who are not members of the Union and all individuals hired after the effective date of this agreement, shall, beginning on the thirtieth (30th) day following the effective date of this agreement or the thirtieth (30th) day following employment, whichever is later, as a condition of employment, either become and remain members of the Union in good standing insofar as the payment of an amount equal to the periodic dues and initiation fees, uniformly required, is concerned, or, in lieu of such Union membership, pay to the Union an equivalent service charge.

2. *Union Dues or Service Charge Deduction Authorization*

(a) The Company, for each of its employees included within the bargaining units recognized by the Company pursuant to Article I hereof, who individually, in writing, duly authorizes his Company Paymaster to do so, will deduct from the earnings payable to such employee on the second pay day of each month, the monthly dues (including initiation fee, if any) for such employee's membership in the Local, or the equivalent service charge, and shall remit promptly to the Local all such deductions. . . .

(b) Subject to applicable law, individual authorizations executed after the effective date of this Agreement shall be signed cards in the form agreed to by the Company and the Union.

ARTICLE III.   WORKING CONDITIONS

1. The Company will continue to provide systematic safety inspections, safety devices, guards, and medical service to minimize accidents and health hazards on its premises.

ARTICLE IV.   DISCRIMINATION AND COERCION

1. Neither the Company nor any of its Foremen, Superintendents, or other agents or representatives, shall discriminate against any employee because such employee is a member, Steward, Officer, or other agent or representative of the Union or of any Local.

2. Neither the Union nor any Local, nor any Steward, Officer, or other agent or representative of either, shall intimidate or coerce any

employee, nor solicit members or funds in the plant during working hours.

3. (a) The Company, the Union and its IUE Locals shall not discriminate against any employee on account of race, color, sex, creed, marital status, age or national origin.

(b) The Company, the Union and its IUE Locals shall not discriminate against any employee because of physical or mental disability or because he or she is a disabled veteran or veteran of the Vietnam era in regard to any position for which the employee is qualified.

ARTICLE XI.   REDUCTION OR INCREASE IN FORCES

1. Whenever there is a reduction in the working force or employees are laid off from their regular jobs, total length of seniority, applied on a plant, department, or other basis as negotiated locally, shall be the major factor determining the employees to be laid off or transferred (exclusive of upgrading or transfers to higher rated jobs). However, ability will be given consideration.

Similarly, in all cases of rehiring after layoff, total length of seniority, applied on a plant, department, or other basis as negotiated locally, shall be the major factor covering such rehiring if the employee is able to do the available work in a satisfactory manner after a minimum amount of training.

ARTICLE XIII.   GRIEVANCE PROCEDURE

1. Grievances may be filed by an employee or group of employees, a Steward or the Local. Grievances of a general nature filed by the Local shall be initiated at the second step of the grievance procedure.

2. *Steps.* Grievances other than those of a general nature may be processed only by recourse to the following successive steps:

(a) *Step One (Foreman Level)*

(1) Within a reasonable time after the occurrence or knowledge of the situation, condition or action of Management giving rise to the grievance, the employee affected thereby or his Steward may present the grievance to the employee's Foreman or other immediate supervisor. (If presented by the employee, he may also have his Steward present.)

(2) Within one working day after such presentation, such Foreman or other immediate supervisor shall give to such employee and Steward his decision with respect to such grievance, or shall advise

them that additional time for such decision is needed, in which event he shall give them such decision within one week thereafter.

(3) A Steward who submits a written grievance to his Foreman shall receive, upon request, a written reply.

(4) If a settlement is not reached between the Steward and his immediate supervisor, the Local may refer the grievance to two representatives of the Local for discussion in the department with representatives of local management for settlement, if possible.

(b) *Step Two (Management Level)*

(1) If a settlement is not reached at Step One, the designated Local official may present to a representative designated by local management, a written statement of such grievance within thirty (30) days of the Company answer at Step One of the grievance procedure giving all pertinent information relative to the grievance and indicating the relief requested, provided, however, that the designated Local official may advise local management that additional time is needed, in which case the Local shall have an additional one week to process the grievance to Step Two. The time limit between Step One and Step Two may be extended by mutual agreement.

(2) Meetings between representatives of the Local and local management shall be arranged at mutually agreeable times for the purpose of discussing such grievances. In those cases where it is mutually agreed by Management and Local representatives that an inspection of the job would be helpful in settling the case, a subcommittee of the Local with Management representatives shall be allowed to make an inspection of the job. Local representatives may include the Business Agent or his assistant or officers of the Local.

Grievances referred to Step Two will be scheduled and discussed as expeditiously as possible but not later than forty-five (45) days after the grievance has been presented to Step Two. Such time limits may be extended by mutual agreement.

(3) Upon request, local management will give the Local a written reply, such reply generally to be issued within two weeks following discussion of the grievance on the merits at the Second Step. Any extension necessary to issue a written reply shall be limited to two weeks.

(c) *Step Three (Headquarters Level)*

(1) Any grievance, having been processed through Step Two without satisfactory settlement, may be referred to the National Officers of the Union for submission to an Executive Officer of the Company or his designated representative, who shall arrange meetings for the purpose of discussing such grievances.

Such grievances shall be submitted to the Company not less than two weeks prior to the date of any discussion and not more than three months after the completion of discussions and the final decision of local management at Step Two.

When the Union requests an emergency meeting on a particular grievance or grievances, such a meeting shall take place within one week after the Company receives the request for such an emergency meeting.

The Company shall give its final decision to the Union in writing within a reasonable time after the completion of discussion on any grievance.

The discussions provided for above may, by mutual agreement, be held at the plant location of the Local submitting the grievance, if requested by the Union. . . .

3. Discipline Based on Warning Notices

Before imposing a disciplinary penalty or discharge which is based upon the cumulative effect of written warning notices, the Company will notify the employee concerned one week in advance. The matter may be made a subject for grievance discussions, but such discussions shall not prevent imposition of the penalty pending their final outcome, and in the event it is determined that an employee has been improperly penalized, he will be reimbursed for any loss of wages sustained as a result of the imposition of the penalty.

ARTICLE XIV. STRIKES AND LOCKOUTS

1. There shall be no strike, sit-down, slowdown, employee demonstration or any other organized or concerted interference with work of any kind in connection with any matter subject to the grievance procedure, and no such interference with work shall be directly or indirectly authorized or sanctioned by a Local or the Union, or their respective Officers or Stewards, unless and until all of the respective provisions of the successive steps of the grievance procedure set forth in Article XIII shall have been complied with by the Local and the Union. The foregoing exception will not apply if (a) the matter is submitted to arbitration as provided in Article XV, or (b) 12 months shall have elapsed after receipt by the Union of the Company's final decision on the grievance at Step Three, or (c) the Company shall not have received written or telegraphic notice of such strike from the Local more than 24 hours prior to

the commencement of such strike, which notice will specify the exhausted grievance over which the strike is being called. Upon receipt by the Company of such a strike notice, the Company and the Union will meet immediately to discuss the dispute and the contemplated action so that management may assess the situation.

2. The Company will not lock out any employee or transfer any job under dispute from the local Works, nor will the local management take similar action while a disputed job is under discussion at any of the steps of the grievance procedure set forth in Article XIII, or if the matter is submitted to arbitration as provided in Article XV.

ARTICLE XV.   ARBITRATION

1. Any grievance which remains unsettled after having been fully processed pursuant to the provisions of Article XIII, and which involves either,

(a) the interpretation or application of a provision of the Agreement, or

(b) a disciplinary penalty (including discharge) imposed on or after the effective date of this Agreement, which is alleged to have been imposed without just cause, or

(c) a nondisciplinary termination occurring after the effective date of this agreement,

may be submitted to arbitration upon written request of either the Union or the Company, provided such request is made within 60 days after the final decision of the Company has been given to the Union pursuant to Article XIII, Section 2(c). For the purpose of proceedings within the scope of (b) above, the standard to be applied by an arbitrator to cases involving disciplinary penalties (including discharge) is that such penalties shall be imposed only for just cause.

2. (a) A request for arbitration shall state in reasonable detail the nature of the dispute and the remedy requested. A copy of the request shall be sent to the American Arbitration Association.

(b) Within 30 days after receipt of a request to arbitrate, the receiving party will give its response thereto in writing, with a copy to the Association, stating whether or not it believes the stated dispute to be arbitrable. If the receiving party believes the dispute not to be arbitrable, it will state its reasons in reasonable detail.

(c) If the response agrees to the arbitrability of the dispute, the Association will proceed to process the request in accordance with Section 3.

(d) If a response to a request for arbitration disagrees as to arbitrability of the dispute, either party may request a conference to discuss the arbitrability of the dispute, and to seek to resolve the differences between the parties.

3. (a) When a request for arbitration involves only relief from a disciplinary penalty or discharge alleged to have been imposed without just cause, or involves a dispute which the Company admits to be arbitrable, or when a final court judgment shall have ordered arbitration of a request, the Association shall submit the appropriate matter promptly to one of the Contract Arbitrators listed below for scheduling of a hearing thereon.

The Contract Arbitrators shall serve for the duration of this Agreement. The Association will assign each arbitration case in rotation, in the order of Contract Arbitrators listed below. If a Contract Arbitrator states that he is unable to accept a case, it will be referred to the next Contract Arbitrator in line.

Whenever the number of unresolved arbitration requests assigned to a Contract Arbitrator shall exceed three, any additional requests which would otherwise be assigned him in order of rotation shall be referred to the next Contract Arbitrator in line.

[List of Contract Arbitrators (23) omitted.—EDS.]

(c) In the conduct of an arbitration hearing, the applicable provisions of the Voluntary Labor Arbitration Rules of the Association shall control, except that either party may, if it desires, be represented by counsel.

(d) The dispute as stated in the request for arbitration shall constitute the sole and entire subject matter to be heard by the arbitrator, unless the parties agree to modify the scope of the hearing.

4. (a) In the event the receiving party has asserted that the dispute contained in a request for arbitration is not arbitrable, the Association shall have authority to process the request for arbitration and appoint an arbitrator in accordance with the procedure set forth in Section 3 above only after a final judgment of a court has determined that the grievance upon which arbitration has been requested raises arbitrable issues and has directed arbitration of such issues. The foregoing part of this section shall not be applicable if the request for arbitration involves only relief from a disciplinary penalty or discharge alleged to have been imposed without just cause.

(b) In the consideration and decision of any question involving arbitrability (including any application to a court for an order directing arbitration), it is the specific agreement of the parties that:

(i) Some types of grievance disputes which may arise during the term of this Agreement shall be subject to arbitration as a matter of right, enforceable in court, at the demand of either party. (See Section 6 below.)

(ii) Other types of disputes shall be subject only to voluntary arbitration, i.e., can be arbitrated only if both parties agree in writing, in the case of each dispute, to do so. (See Section 7 below.)

(iii) This Agreement sets out expressly all the restrictions and obligations assumed by the respective parties, and no implied restrictions or obligations [are] inherent in this Agreement or were assumed by the parties in entering into this Agreement.

(iv) In the consideration of whether a matter is subject to arbitration as a matter of right, a fundamental principle shall be that the Company retains all its rights to manage the business, including (but not limited to) the right to determine the methods and means by which its operations are to be carried on, to direct the work force and to conduct its operations in a safe and effective manner, subject only to the express limitations set forth in this National Agreement, Local Seniority Supplements executed under the provisions of Article XI thereof, and Local Understandings executed in accordance with Section 3 of Article XXI thereof; and it is understood that the parties have not agreed to arbitrate demands which challenge action taken by the Company in the exercise of any such rights, except where such challenge is based upon a violation of any such express limitations (other than those set out in Section 7 below).

(v) No matter will be considered arbitrable unless it is found that the parties clearly agreed that the subject involved would be arbitrable in light of the principles of arbitrability set forth in this Article and no court or arbitrator shall or may proceed under any presumption that a request to arbitrate is arbitrable.

(c) If a final judgment of a court has determined that a request raises arbitrable issues, the court's decision shall specify in reasonable detail the issues as to which arbitration is directed. The arbitration shall thereafter proceed only upon the issues specified in such final court judgment and the arbitrator shall have no authority or jurisdiction to consider issues other than those specified.

5. The powers of an arbitrator shall include the authority to render a final and binding decision with respect to any dispute brought before him including the right to modify or reduce or rescind any disciplinary action taken by the Company but excluding the right to amend, modify or alter the terms of this Agreement, or any Local Understanding.

The expense of the arbitration will be borne equally by both parties.

Individuals who are covered by this Agreement do not have the right to invoke the arbitration procedure on their own initiative. The arbitration procedure can only be invoked by the Company on its behalf or the Union on behalf of the employees.

6. (a) Arbitration as a matter of right includes only requests to arbitrate which involve:

(i) Disciplinary action (including discharge) or nondisciplinary terminations but with certain exceptions spelled out in this article;

(ii) The claimed violation of a specific provision or provisions of the National Agreement (with the limitations and exceptions set out in this Article);

(iii) The claimed violation of a provision or provisions of a signed Local Seniority Supplement entered into in accordance with Article XI, Section 2 of this National Agreement or of a provision or provisions of a Local Understanding entered into in accordance with Article XXI, Section 3 of this National Agreement.

(b) A request for arbitration, in order to be subject to arbitration as a matter of right under the provisions of Subsections (a)(ii) and (a)(iii) above, must allege a direct violation of the express purpose of the contractual provision in question, rather than of an indirect or implied purpose. For example, a request which claims incorrect application of the method of computing overtime pay under the provisions of Section 2 of Article V would be arbitrable as a matter of right, whereas a request which questioned the right of the Company to require the performance of reasonable overtime work, on the claimed ground that Article V contains an implied limitation of that right, would be subject only to voluntary arbitration. A request that Article XI and the appropriate Local Seniority Supplement had been violated by the layoff of a senior employee in preference to a junior employee would be arbitrable as a matter of right but a request that subcontracting of work in the plant while bargaining unit employees are on layoff violated a claimed implied limitation of Article XI and the applicable Local Seniority Supplement would be subject only to voluntary arbitration.

7. All requests for arbitration which are not subject to arbitration as a matter of right under the provisions of Section 6 above, are subject only to voluntary arbitration. In particular, it is specifically agreed that arbitration requests shall be subject only to voluntary arbitration, by mutual agreement, if they . . . [i]nvolve discipline or discharge imposed on employees having less than six months of service credits with the Company . . . .

9. Any arbitration case between the Company and the Union which is limited to a disciplinary penalty other than discharge is covered by the supplemental arbitration procedure set forth below:

(a) The following rules shall apply in cases covered by this section:

(i) The only issue before the arbitrator shall be whether the discipline was imposed for just cause.

(ii) There shall be no transcript of the hearing.

(iii) There shall be no post-hearing briefs or other written arguments by the parties.

(iv) If either party so requests, there shall be a thirty (30) minute recess before any closing oral argument by the parties.

(v) The arbitrator shall render an Award without an Opinion no more than twenty-four (24) hours after the closing of the oral hearing.

(b) The compensation for an arbitrator for hearing a case under this procedure shall be a fee of $650.00 for each case. The arbitrator shall also be entitled to travel expenses in accordance with the regular procedures of the American Arbitration Association.

(c) A special panel of arbitrators shall be established to hear cases under this procedure by mutual agreement of the parties.

(d) Whenever a request for arbitration meets the criteria set forth above, the Association shall designate an arbitrator from the special panel of arbitrators, as provided for herein, to hear the case instead of a regular Contract Arbitrator, as provided for in Section 3(a) of this Article, as follows: . . .

(ii) A date for a hearing shall be scheduled within sixty (60) days of the appointment of the arbitrator.

ARTICLE XXI.   LOCAL UNDERSTANDINGS

1. The provisions of this Agreement are subject to all present local understandings, and such understandings will remain in effect unless changed in the manner provided in the following section.

2. After the effective date of this Agreement, new local understandings will be recognized and made effective only where set forth in writing and signed by local management and the Local, and approved by the Company and the Union.

3. The existence of, or any alleged violation of, a local understanding shall not be the basis of any arbitration proceeding, unless such understanding is in writing and signed by the Company and Union.

ARTICLE XXII.   JOB AND INCOME SECURITY

1. *Definitions*

(a) The terms "plant closing" and "to close a plant" mean the announcement and carrying out of a plan to terminate and discontinue either all Company operations at any plant, service shop, or other facility, or those Company operations which would result in the termination of all employees represented by the Union at that location when those employees do not have displacement rights.

Such terms do not refer to the termination and discontinuance of only part of the Company's operations at any plant, service shop, or other facility (except as specifically provided in the paragraph above) nor to the termination or discontinuance of all of its former operations coupled with the announced intention to commence there either larger or smaller other operations. Any employees released by such latter changes will be considered as out for lack of work and will be subject to provisions applicable to those on layoff.

Also, such terms do not refer to the transfer or sale of such operations to a successor employer who offers continued employment to Company employees. Company employees who are not offered continued employment by the Company or by the successor employer will be considered as out for lack of work and will be subject to provisions applicable to those on layoff. . . .

(c) The terms "transfer of work," "to transfer work," and "work transfer" mean the discontinuance of ongoing work at one location coupled with the assignment of the same work to a different location, including subcontracting the same work to another employer, if such assignment of work would directly cause a decrease in the number of represented employees performing such work at the first location. . . .

2. *Plant Closing*

(a) *General*

(1) Whenever the Company decides to close a plant, the Company shall give notice of its decision to the Union, the Local or Locals involved, and the employees concerned. Thereafter, as the Company, in the course of such plant closing, no longer has need for the work then being done by an employee, his employment by the Company may be terminated, subject to compliance with the provisions of this Section 2.

(2) Each employee shall be given at least one week's advance notice of the specific date of his termination.

(b) *Severance Pay*

(1) An eligible employee whose employment is terminated because of plant closing shall be entitled to Severance Pay in a lump sum, for which he is eligible as described below and the full vacation allowance for which he might have qualified for the calendar year in which his employment is terminated and any other accumulated allowances due him . . . .

(6) *Computation of Severance Pay*

(i) An employee with one or more but less than fifteen years of continuous service will, in accordance with the provisions set forth above, be eligible for Severance Pay computed on the basis of one and 1/2 week's pay for each of the employee's full years of continuous service plus 3/8 of a week's pay for each additional 3 months of continuous service at the time of termination; provided that the amount of the Severance Pay benefit as computed under this paragraph shall be subject to a minimum benefit equal to 4 weeks' pay.

(ii) An employee with fifteen or more years of continuous service will, in accordance with the provisions set forth above, be eligible for Severance Pay computed on the basis of two weeks' pay for each of the employee's full years of continuous service plus 1/2 of a week's pay for each additional 3 months of continuous service at the time of termination.

3. *Retraining and Readjustment Assistance* . . .

(e) *Preferential Placement*

(1) *Eligibility.* An hourly rated or nonexempt salaried employee eligible for: (i) Severance Pay under Section 2 or (ii) Income Extension Aid ("IEA") resulting from being displaced and subject to layoff in the immediate chain of displacement resulting when a job is directly eliminated by a transfer of work, the discontinuation of a discrete, unreplaced product line, the introduction of a robot, or the introduction of an automated manufacturing or office machine may elect, prior to the employee's termination for plant closing or layoff, and up to thirty (30) days thereafter (except where the laid off employee has elected to receive his IEA in lump sum), to be placed in a Preferential Placement status.

(2) *Election Procedure.* To elect Preferential Placement the employee shall designate up to five (5) domestic General Electric Company manufacturing plant, service shop or distribution center locations on forms provided exclusively by the Company. . . .

(3) *Placement Standard.* Individuals in Preferential Placement status will be given preference, to the extent practical, over new hires for job openings at the locations designated by them in order of their length of continuity of service when they possess the necessary job qualifications established by the hiring location. . . .

(5) *Seniority.* Individuals placed or reemployed under this Section 3(e) will have seniority for the purpose of subsequent layoff, recall, upgrading and other seniority purposes at their new location based upon the established seniority procedures and practices at their new location. While working at a designated location as a result of Preferential Placement, an employee will not be eligible for recall to his old location.

4. *Income Extension Aid*

(a) *Computation of Income Extension Aid*
(1) An employee with one or more years of continuous service will, in accordance with the provisions hereinafter set forth, have available Income Extension Aid computed on the basis of one week's pay for each of the employee's full years of continuous service plus 1/4 of a week's pay for each additional 3 months of continuous service at the time of layoff. . . .

(3) *Minimum Benefit.* The amount of the Income Extension Aid benefit as computed under Section 4(a)(1) shall be subject to a minimum benefit equal to 4 weeks' pay. . . .

(b) *Benefits Available at Layoff*
. . . Prior to the exhaustion of his entitlements to federal and state unemployment compensation benefits, the weekly payment shall be in that amount (if any) which, when added to the total federal and state unemployment compensation benefits received for that week, equals seventy-five percent of his weekly pay . . . .

After exhaustion of his entitlements to federal and state unemployment compensation benefits, the weekly payment shall be in that amount which equals seventy-five percent of his weekly pay . . . . Payments shall be made only if the employee certifies that he is still unemployed and they shall continue only until the full amount for which the employee qualifies under Section 4(a) is paid. . . .

5. *Notice, Bargaining and Information Requirements*

This Section sets forth the full obligations of the Company with regard to notice, bargaining with and information to the Union concerning plant closing, work transfer, subcontracting and the installation of robots or automated manufacturing or office machines.

(a) *Plant Closing*

(1) *Notice.* The Company will give notice of its intent to close a manufacturing plant, service shop or distribution center a minimum of one year in advance of the plant closing date to the Union, the Local involved and to employees concerned. Such notice will include identification of the plant to be closed, the Local involved and the date when terminations of represented employees because of the plant closing are expected to begin.

(2) *Bargaining.* If the Local requests decision bargaining within ten (10) working days following a Company notice of intent to close a manufacturing plant, service shop, or distribution center, the Company will be available to meet with the Local within five (5) working days of such request and the bargaining period shall continue for up to forty-five (45) calendar days from the date of the Company notice of intent to close the plant unless this period is extended by mutual agreement. The Company will make a decision whether or not to close the plant after this bargaining period.

(3) *Information.* If information is requested by the Local for bargaining provided for in Section 5(a)(2) of this Article, the Company will promptly make the following information available to the Local for such bargaining. This information will specifically include the express reason(s) for intending to close the plant and, where employment cost is a significant factor, the related wages, payroll allowances and employee benefits expenses of represented employees at the plant intended to be closed. This information will be treated as confidential by the Local.

(b) *Transfer of Ongoing Production Work*

(1) *Notice.* The Company will give notice of its intent to transfer ongoing production work a minimum of six (6) months in advance of the effective date of the work transfer to the Local involved. Such notice will include identification of the work to be transferred, the expected decrease in the number of represented employees as a direct consequence of the transfer of work and the anticipated date of the transfer of work.

(2) *Bargaining.* [Deleted: similar to §5(a)(2) above — EDS.]

(3) *Information.* [Deleted: similar to §5(a)(3) above — EDS.]

(c) *Transfer of Nonproduction Work*

(1) *Notice.* The Company will give notice of its intent to transfer nonproduction work, or subcontract nonproduction work at the same plant location or elsewhere if such subcontracting of work would directly cause a decrease in the number of represented employees performing such work, a minimum of sixty (60) calendar days in advance of the effective date of the work transfer or subcontracting to the Local involved. In the case of transfers of work or subcontracting that would directly cause a decrease of more than 50 represented employees performing such work, the notice period will be six (6) months. Such notice will include identification of the work to be transferred or subcontracted, the expected decrease in the number of represented employees as a direct consequence of the transfer of work or subcontracting and the anticipated date of the transfer of work or subcontracting.

(2) *Bargaining.* [Deleted: similar to §5(a)(2) above — EDS.]

(3) *Information.* [Deleted: similar to §5(a)(3) above — EDS.] . . .

(e) *Installation of Robots or Automated Manufacturing or Office Machines*

With respect to the installation of robots or automated manufacturing or office machines, the Company will give a minimum of sixty (60) days' notice to the Local involved before the use of a robot or an automated manufacturing or office machine in a work area. Such notice will include a description of the function of the device, identification of the work involved, the expected decrease in the number of represented employees as a direct consequence of the use of the device and the anticipated date of the use of the device.

(f) The Company will notify the Local of its decision to utilize a subcontractor to perform work of the type regularly performed by bargaining unit employees, where the work will be done by a subcontractor at another location and there is no decrease in the number of represented employees performing like work. The notice will give a general description of the work and state the express reasons for subcontracting the work.

6. *Job Preservation* . . .

(b) *Job Preservation Steering Committee*

The Company recognizes the importance of job security to the Union and acknowledges that subcontracting work and the introduction of enhanced technology, while enabling the Company to succeed in the many competitive environments in which it operates, may result in a decrease in General Electric Company jobs. In order to balance competitive realities with the Union's interest in protecting jobs, the Company and Union will establish a joint Job Preservation Steering Committee at each Company location employing over 50 bargaining unit employees to meet and discuss issues such as:

- Opportunities for job creation
- Potential outsourcing/subcontracting and work transfers, including situations where there is no direct decrease in the number of represented employees
- Training for anticipated technology changes
- Work practices and local agreements to increase efficiency
- Investment plans and potential impact on jobs

... This Steering Committee structure is not intended to displace the workings of other ongoing union-management activities, including the grievance procedure and the decision bargaining provisions of Article XXII, which exist at each plant location. . . .

The Company and the Union recognize the value of holding periodic meetings at the business level to discuss the state of the business and future plans that may impact employees represented by the Union. To that end, the Company and the Union will develop a process to conduct semi-annual meetings at the business level for this purpose. . . .

8. *Lump Sum Payments*

Service credits previously accumulated, continuity of service, and recall rights will be lost upon receipt by the employee of . . . special termination payments under this Article, or payment of Severance Pay under the Plant Closing Section 2. . . .

10. *Other*

The provisions of this article shall not be applicable where the Company decides to close a plant or lay off an employee because of the Company's inability to secure production, or carry on its operations, as a consequence of a strike, slowdown, or other interference with or interruption [of] work participated in by employees in a Company plant, service shop, or other facility. However, the operation of this section shall not affect the rights or benefits already provided hereunder to an employee laid off for lack of work prior to the commencement of any such strike, interference, or interruption.

11. *[Grievances]*

A grievance arising under this article may be processed in accordance with the grievance procedure set forth in Article XIII. However, no matter or controversy concerning the provisions of this article or the interpretation or application thereof shall be subject to arbitration under the provisions of Article XV hereof, except by mutual agreement.

ARTICLE XXVIII.   UPGRADING AND JOB POSTING

1. *Standard for Filling Open Jobs and Upgrading*

The Company will, to the extent practical, give first consideration for job openings and upgrading to present employees, when employees with the necessary qualifications are available. In upgrading employees to higher rated jobs, the Company will take into consideration as an important factor, the relative length of seniority of the employees who it finds are qualified for such upgrading . . . .

ARTICLE XXX.   ISSUES OF GENERAL APPLICATION

This Agreement, the 2000-2003 Settlement Agreement, the 2000-2003 Wage Agreement, and the 2000-2003 Pension and Insurance Agreement between the parties are intended to be and shall be in full settlement of all issues which were the subject of collective bargaining between the parties in national level collective bargaining negotiations in 2000. Consequently, it is agreed that none of such issues shall be subject to collective bargaining during the term of this Agreement and there shall be no strike or lockout in connection with any such issue or issues; provided, however, that this provision shall not be construed to limit or modify the rights of the parties hereto under . . . Article XIV of this Agreement.

ARTICLE XXXI.   DURATION OF AGREEMENT

This National Agreement shall be effective as of June 26, 2000, between the Company, the Union, and each of the IUE (AFL-CIO) Locals now certified as the representative of Company employees, as set forth in the Preamble to this Agreement, and shall continue in full force and effect to and including the 15th day of June, 2003, and from year to year thereafter unless modified or terminated as hereinafter provided.

ARTICLE XXXII.   MODIFICATION AND TERMINATION

(a) Either the Company or the Union may terminate this National Agreement by written notice to the other not more than ninety days and not less than sixty days prior to June 15, 2003, or prior to June 15 of any subsequent year. Not more than 15 days following receipt of such notice, collective bargaining negotiations shall commence between the parties for the purpose of considering the terms of a new agreement, and a proposal for a revision of wages which may be submitted by either the Company or the Union.

(b) If either the Company or the Union desires to modify this National Agreement, it shall, not more than ninety days and not less than sixty days prior to June 15, 2003, or prior to June 15 of any subsequent year, so notify the other in writing. Not more than 15 days following receipt of such notice, collective bargaining negotiations shall commence between the parties for the purpose of considering changes in this National Agreement, and a proposal for revision of wages which may be submitted by either the Company or the Union.

If settlement is not reached by June 15, 2003, or prior to June 15 of any subsequent year, this National Agreement shall continue in full force and effect until the tenth day following written notice given by either the Company or the Union of its intention to terminate such Agreement, during which time there shall be no strike or lockout.

Dated: June 26, 2000

2000 Memorandum of Agreement Between Saturn and the UAW — Selected Provisions

1. PREAMBLE

This Memorandum of Agreement (Agreement) is entered into between Saturn Corporation (Saturn), a wholly-owned subsidiary of General Motors Corporation (GM) and the International Union, United Automobile, Aerospace and Agricultural Implement Workers of American (Union). Saturn and the Union have long recognized the need for a new approach to Union/Management relations and the more effective use of human resources in the manufacture of small cars in the United States. Since GM and the Union first met and authorized the establishment of a study center and the creation of the Corporation, the parties recognize that the global competitiveness in the auto industry has significantly increased. GM and the Union further recognize the necessity of further developing this innovative approach to Union/Management relations and the necessary staffing to accomplish our mutual objectives. General Motors, Saturn Corporation and the Union understand fully the necessity to successfully forge a renewed commitment to a cooperative problem solving relationship and demonstrate that a competitive, world class, quality vehicle will be developed and manufactured in the United States with a represented work force. It is in this renewed spirit of mutual respect and recognition of each other's stakes and equities that this Agreement is entered into and agreed upon.

2. RECOGNITION

From the outset, Saturn has been and is, a joint effort of both Union and Management. The success of Saturn is fully dependent on its people. Hiring and retention of experienced, dedicated personnel is essential. It is recognized that the best source of such trained automotive workers is found in the existing GM-UAW workforce. Therefore, to insure a fully qualified workforce, a majority of the full initial complement of operating and skilled technicians in Saturn will come from GM-UAW units throughout the United States.

The UAW is recognized as the bargaining agent for the operating and skilled technicians within Saturn.

3. Union Representation During Bridging Period

During any bridging period, the Vice President of the GM Department, UAW, will appoint representatives to work jointly with the Saturn organization. The International Union will charter separate Union locals to represent Saturn members.

4. Union Membership and Check-Off

To the extent permitted by law, within ten (10) days after the thirtieth (30th) day following hire by Saturn, all bargaining unit members shall become and shall remain members of the Union to the extent of paying an initiation fee and membership dues specified by the International Union.

Saturn will agree to provide for check-off of union dues and initiation fees. The Union will agree to indemnify Saturn with respect to any claims arising out of the check-off provisions.

5. Current GM-UAW National Agreement

This separate, free-standing, Agreement will cover bargaining unit Saturn members. The provisions of the current or any subsequent GM-UAW National Agreement will have no bearing on Saturn unless adopted by agreement between Saturn and the Union.

6. Saturn People Philosophy Summary Statement

We believe that all people want to be involved in decisions that affect them, care about their jobs and each other, take pride in themselves and in their contributions and want to share in the success of their efforts.

7. Saturn Corporation Philosophy

Fundamental to the Saturn philosophy is the shared belief that meeting the needs of people, customers, Saturn members, suppliers, retailers and neighbors is fundamental to fulfilling the Saturn mission.

8. MISSION

The mission of Saturn is to market vehicles developed and manufactured in the United States that are world leaders in quality, cost and customer enthusiasm through the integration of people, technology and business systems.

Consistent with being quality and cost competitive, a goal of Saturn is to utilize American-made components in assembly of its vehicles.

9. SYMBOLS

Saturn believes that symbols should be positive to promote our philosophy and culture. Saturn and the Union will strive to achieve positive symbols that minimize the differentiation between people in the elements of a successful organization, such as methods of pay, purchase of GM products, common cafeterias, parking, identification, entrances, lack of time clocks, etc. To the degree possible, recognizing the need to remain competitive, consistency of treatment for everyone (represented and non-represented) will be an important objective for Saturn.

10. STRUCTURE AND DECISION-MAKING PROCESS

The structure of Saturn reflects certain basic principles, e.g., recognition of the stakes and equities of everyone in the organization; full participation by the Union; use of a consensus decision-making process; placement of authority and decision-making in the most appropriate part of the organization, with emphasis on the Work Unit; and, free flow of information and clear definition of the decision-making process.

As guided by these principles, the organization will be structured in the following way:

Structure:

WORK UNIT MEMBER
The individual Saturn member.

WORK UNIT
An integrated group of approximately 8-12 Work Unit members.

WORK UNIT MODULE
A grouping of Work Units interrelated as to geography, product or technology.

BUSINESS UNITS
An integrated group of Work Units and Work Unit Modules representing common areas.

MANUFACTURING ACTION COUNCIL (MAC)
An integrated group of Business Units comprising the entire manufacturing and assembly complex, at a given site location.

TECHNICAL DEVELOPMENT ACTION COUNCIL (TDAC)
An Integrated Business Unit comprising the Advanced product and Manufacturing Engineering Functions, at a given site location.

STRATEGIC ACTION COUNCIL (SAC)
Will have particular concern for long range goals and health of Saturn, with particular emphasis on planning and outside interested parties, including retailers, suppliers, communities, stockholders, etc. Composition of the SAC will be determined with appropriate input from Saturn and the Union.

The Structure also provides for:

UAW WORK UNIT COUNSELOR
Will be elected by the members in the Unit or jointly selected by the Parties and will represent the Union and Saturn in the Work Unit; the current manner and process for such election will remain in effect until a mutually agreed upon selection process is established by the Parties. The Counselor is a working member of the Work Unit.

UAW COORDINATOR
Will be elected; the manner and process determined by the Union. The UAW Coordinator will serve as administrator of the Agreement on behalf of and for the Union.

UAW SKILLED TRADES UNIT ADVISOR

Will be elected; the manner and process determined by the Union. The UAW Skilled Trades Advisor will serve as administrator of the Agreement on behalf of and for the Union.

UAW BUSINESS UNIT ADVISOR

Will be elected at large; the manner and process for such election to be determined by the Union. The UAW Business Unit Advisor will serve as administrator of the Agreement on behalf of and for the Union.

UAW MAC ADVISOR

Will be elected at large; the manner and process for such election to be determined by the Union. The UAW MAC Advisor represents the Union and its members as part of the MAC consensus decision-making body. The UAW MAC Advisor serves as the highest local administrator of the Agreement, and as a communication link with the UAW SAC Advisor.

UAW TDAC ADVISOR

Will be elected at large; the manner and process for such election to be determined by the Union. The UAW TDAC Advisor represents the Union and its members as part of the TDAC consensus decision-making body. The UAW TDAC Advisor serves as the highest Local administrator of the Agreement, and as a communication link with the UAW SAC Advisor.

UAW SAC ADVISOR

There will be Union representation on the SAC selected by the Union. The manner and process of such selection will be determined by the Union.

Function

Saturn will be unique in the manner in which the basic building blocks, the Work Units, will operate. Consensus decision-making will be utilized with a strong focus on both current and near term decisions. These Work Units will be self-managed, integrated horizontally and reflect synergistic group growth. These Units will have responsibilities to manage such functions as producing to schedule, producing a quality product, performing to budget, housekeeping, health, safety and ergonomics, maintenance of equipment, material and inventory control, training, job assignment, repairs, scrap control and absenteeism. They will hold meetings, obtain supplies, keep records, seek resources as needed, and be responsible for their job preparation. They will constantly seek improvement in quality, cost and work environment.

The Work Unit will also be responsible for the planning and the scheduling of the work and communications within and outside the group.

The Module will be responsible for selection decisions for acceptance into the Work Units. Appropriate criteria will be used in making such decisions by utilizing a hiring team consisting of both represented and non-represented module leadership and elected union representation.

The Business Unit will do advanced planning for resources both short and near term. The Business Units will be composed of all Work Unit Advisors. The Business Units will determine the resources needed by the Work Units, including administration, engineering, materials, financial, etc.

The Manufacturing Action Council (MAC) will be responsible for living the Saturn philosophy to insure success of the mission. It will provide the resources needed by the Business Units on a timely and cost effective basis.

In addition, the MAC will represent and protect the interests, stakes and equities of the Business Units and the Work Unit members, coordinate the activities of and provide information to the Business Units, appraise the performance of the entire organization, and serve as a link to Saturn as a whole.

The Technical Development Action Council (TDAC) will be responsible for living the Saturn philosophy to insure success of the mission. It will provide the resources needed by the Business Unit on a timely and cost effective basis.

In addition, the TDAC will represent and protect the interests, stakes, and equities of the Business Unit and the Work Unit members, coordinate the activities of and provide information to the Business Unit, appraise the performance of the entire organization, and serve as a link to Saturn as a whole.

The Strategic Action Council (SAC) will undertake the strategic business planning necessary to assure the long-term viability of the enterprise, and will be responsive to the needs of the marketplace relative to quality, cost and timing. The SAC will obtain, maintain, and replace the resources necessary to meet the mission in concert with the philosophy. It is charged with creating the environment, facilities, tools, education and support systems which will enable Saturn members to perform their responsibilities.

11. CONSENSUS GUIDELINES

The structure described in Section 10 is intended to make the Union a full partner in Saturn. The consensus technique is the basic support methodology for Saturn decision-making and conflict resolution processes. The parties agree that the consensus process, as outlined below, is the primary method for making decisions and resolving disagreements.

In the context of Saturn's philosophy and mission, decisions and disagreements will be resolved within the following guidelines:

- Resolution is achieved through the joint efforts of the parties in discovering the "best" solution.
- The solution must provide a high level of acceptance for all parties.
- Once agreement is reached, the parties must be totally committed to the solution.
- Any of the parties may block a potential decision. However, the party blocking the decision must search for alternatives.
- In the event an alternative solution is not forthcoming, the blocking party must reevaluate the position in the context of the philosophy and mission.
- Voting, "trading" and compromise are not part of this process.
- The joint effort is aimed at discovering the best decision/resolution within the context of Saturn's philosophy and mission while, at the same time, satisfying the stakes and equities of all major stakeholders.

12. SATURN CONFLICT RESOLUTION PROCEDURE

There is a four-step problem solving procedure, the last step of which involves final and binding arbitration. Conflicts may be reinstated in those instances where the International Union, UAW, by its Executive Board, Public Review Board, or Constitutional Convention Appeals Committee finds the conflict was improperly resolved by the Union or the Union representative.

SATURN CONFLICT RESOLUTION

	MANAGEMENT	UAW	PROCESS
Step 1	• Member • Work Unit • Work Unit Counselor • Module Advisor		• Discuss • Seek consensus using conflict resolution model • Obtain resource assistance as required • Discuss with other advisors as necessary
Step 2	Operations Module Advisor Crew Leader Ops/Engineering Maintenance Leader People Systems	UAW MAC Advisor UAW Coordinator UAW Business Unit Advisor UAW MAC/TDAC Advisor	• Timely meeting • Seek consensus using conflict resolution model • Obtain resource[s] as required • If unresolved issue put in writing by UAW Coordinator or UAW Business Unit Advisor or UAW MAC/TDAC Advisor • If unresolved — Management issues written answer
Step 3	People Systems Team Leader (Business Unit or TDAC) People Systems Advisor (MAC)	UAW Business Unit Advisor UAW Skilled Trades Unit Advisor UAW TDAC Advisor UAW MAC Advisor Regional Representative	• Timely meeting • Obtain resources as required • Seek consensus using conflict resolution model • If unresolved — both parties issue written positions
Step 4	UAW/GM DEPT UMPIRE STAFF		• Impartial umpire selected • Cost shared • Issue presented • Decision final and binding

13. EQUAL EMPLOYMENT OPPORTUNITY

The philosophy and mission of Saturn are designed to be in full and complete compliance with the legal and moral principles of equal opportunity in employment. Accordingly, Saturn, the Union, and each and every member of Saturn pledge to treat all persons equally without regard to their race, color, religion, age, sex, national origin, disability or sexual orientation.

14. RECRUITMENT AND SELECTION

The Saturn organization will require people who can fully commit to the philosophy and effectively contribute to its mission. Both parties recognize the critical importance of a process for recruitment and selection which accurately and objectively assesses candidate qualifications. The complexity of such a process supports the establishment of a joint team to work on the development and ultimate implementation of such a process in accordance with guidelines to be established by the parties. In this regard, because of the qualifications and experience of the current GM-UAW workforce, they will be the primary source for the initial complement, up to full capacity, of operating and skilled trades technicians. The parties will actively recruit GM-UAW employees (active and inactive), including communications emphasizing the exciting and unique opportunities available in the Saturn culture. It is understood that Saturn membership is conditional on meeting established recruitment and selection criteria.

The Saturn philosophy requires a dedicated and committed workforce. Accordingly, no active or inactive UAW-represented GM employee will be required to become a Saturn applicant, nor will such employee's refusal of an offer of employment by Saturn impact the employee's benefits under the GM-UAW National Agreement.

16. TRAINING

The success of Saturn in meeting its mission in an internationally competitive environment is dependent upon the continuous development and implementation of new tools, methods and cutting edge technology. Training and education provide the tools necessary for all Saturn team members to meet these ongoing challenges, and programs to meet these goals will be jointly developed and administered. To help assure Saturn's long-term viability, jointly developed competency-based training of all Saturn members is mandatory.

17. JOB DESIGN

In keeping with the Saturn mission and culture, each Work Unit will have the responsibility and authority to produce quality products to schedule at competitive costs. The Units will have responsibility for both direct and indirect work, including training, housekeeping, provision for relief, etc. Individual jobs will be designed with the appropriate resources to develop the optimum balance between people and technology, taking into account health, safety and ergonomic issues, with ongoing responsibility to determine methods to become more competitive.

18. PLANNING AND RELIEF

Job content within the Work Units will be designed to include both direct work and indirect work. Therefore, it is expected that Work Units will be able to handle the personal relief needs of individual Saturn members.

19. CLASSIFICATIONS

Saturn will have a job classification structure for represented members that has the classification of "Operating Technician" to which other than skilled trades members will be assigned, and seven additional classifications to which all skilled trades members will be assigned as identified below:

- Tool & Die
- Machine Repair
- Electrical
- Stationary Engineer
- Assembly Layout (TDAC only)
- Model Maker (TDAC only)
- Model Maker Leader (TDAC only)

20. LENGTH OF SERVICE

New Saturn members will establish a Length of Service date by site location effective with their date of hire. Length of service will be used as a tie-breaker in those unusual situations where competing members are equal in all respects; and, as a trigger point for compensation progression or specifically negotiated benefit coverage.

21. JOB SECURITY

Saturn recognizes that people are the most valuable asset of the organization. It is people who develop new technologies and systems, and people who make these systems work in order to meet Saturn's mission. Accordingly, those Saturn members who are eligible for job security, as defined below, shall not be laid off except in situations which the SAC determines are due to unforeseen or catastrophic events or severe economic conditions. In the event former GM employees (active or laid off) who are required to quit to become Saturn members are laid off because of such events or conditions, the parties will discuss the matter in an attempt to effect an equitable solution, such as separation payments, return to General Motors or reinstatement of GM recall or rehire rights.

A Saturn member will have permanent job security eligibility if either of the following applies to that member:

a. The member quit while an active GM-UAW employee or was hired while on layoff with recall or rehire rights from a GM-UAW unit in the U.S. to join Saturn as part of the full initial complement of operating and skilled technicians in Saturn; or

b. The member is, at any point in time, among the 80% of Saturn members with the longest Saturn Length of Service by site location.

Saturn recognizes the desirability of regular employment and will attempt to avoid laying off members not eligible for job security. In the unlikely event of a layoff at a site location, members will be laid off and recalled by Saturn Length of Service.

22. REWARD SYSTEM

The reward system in Saturn will recognize certain critical elements including the mission and philosophy, the necessity that Saturn be profitable and the principle of risk and reward.

Three basic elements are recognized: base compensation, risk/reward and benefits.

Base Compensation

Saturn members' base compensation is established on an annual salary basis, and they will be paid semi-monthly on the 15th of the month and the last day of the month.

The base compensation for Saturn members was adjusted to 95% of straight time base wages of UAW/GM compensation rates. Base compensation will remain at this level until the complete phase-in of risk/reward. Thereafter, base compensation may be adjusted periodically based on such factors as the general state of the economy, inflation, the competitive situation, etc., by approval of the SAC.

Quarterly Payments

In addition, during the phase-in of risk/reward, a sum will be calculated quarterly reflecting the remaining economics received by a comparable GM/UAW employee including COLA. The total sum generated through this calculation will be distributed to members on a quarterly basis.

Risk/Reward

In addition to the base rate, risk will be 5% and will be paid semi-monthly. It will be based on factors such as:

a. Performance to Objectives of Saturn and Individual Business and Work Units;
b. Achievement of specific objective productivity targets;
c. Saturn sharing formula through which profits will be shared above a specified level of return to Saturn;
d. Quality bonus based on World Class Levels.

The risk/reward system will be designed to provide attainable goals which, if met, will provide compensation equivalent to that earned by comparable employees in GM. Performance above or below those goals would provide greater or lesser compensation than comparable employees in GM. . . .

23. WORKING HOURS

To fulfill the objectives of the Saturn philosophy and mission, it will be necessary to have flexible hours of work that meet the needs of the individual as well as Saturn.

26. SHIFT ASSIGNMENTS IN SATURN

The Saturn philosophy emphasizes equality among all members and the shared sense of belonging to a successful operation in which everyone has common needs and goals. Accordingly the rotating shift approach has been implemented by the parties. The feasibility of introducing fixed shifts or other options will be examined by the parties and presented for consideration by the appropriate Action Council.

27. PERSONAL ABSENCE/LEAVES OF ABSENCE

Absenteeism affects the commitment to Saturn and places an unnecessary burden on fellow team members. Accordingly, programs will be developed to discourage absenteeism and to encourage regular attendance. Provision will be made for both paid and unpaid leaves of absence.

28. CODE OF CONDUCT

The code of conduct for Saturn is established in its mission and philosophy statements, which set forth the basic operating principles of the organization. Actions or behavior that are contrary to these principles may be subject to the Saturn Consultation Process, which will be established by the parties and set out in the Agreement. If counseling and attempts to modify behavior prove ineffective or in instances of severe misconduct, Saturn may initiate disciplinary action or discharge. Complaints concerning discipline or discharge must be filed within three (3) working days of the action to be valid.

29. SATURN CONSULTATION PROCESS

The Consultation Process will include three formal stages: (1) Amber Zone, (2) Red Zone, (3) Decision Day. Members in the Consultation Process will be offered Union Representation to ensure a fair [and] equitable process. In situations where any member's conduct or attitude is adversely affecting the Work Unit, initial corrective action will concentrate on consultation, guidance and review. Such assistance does not affect the basic principle that the individual member is responsible for his/her behavior. The parties agree to work toward a variety of approaches to be followed in the attempt to encourage the member to become a full participant in the unit.

30. STRIKES, STOPPAGES AND LOCKOUTS

The philosophy and mission of Saturn and the unique culture created in the work environment are opposed to unauthorized lockouts, strikes, work stoppages, sit-downs, slow-downs, curtailment of work, restriction or interference with production or facilities, picketing, or similar activities. Further, the parties hereby pledge that no lockouts or strikes will be authorized without full and complete compliance with the Procedure to Modify the Agreement contained herein.

32. Components Manufacturing

Many decisions are yet to be made regarding the integration of the Saturn complex which were reviewed and discussed during the Agreement process. As these issues arise in the future, the parties agree to review the specifics of the component part(s) being considered to determine if Saturn can be competitive in quality and cost.

33. Procedure to Modify the Agreement

Once an Agreement is ratified and becomes effective, it will remain in full force and effect unless modified by the parties. However, in the event the parties wish to conduct formal negotiations on an entire Agreement once a full complement of members has been hired, such negotiations will be concluded no later than six months after the commencement of steady state as described herein. The parties are specifically empowered to make mutually satisfactory modifications, additions or deletions to the Agreement which are in line with the philosophy and mission of Saturn on an ongoing basis. In the event either party is unable to secure agreement on a modification(s) it desires, such party may institute this Procedure to Modify the Agreement.

A.   Notice of Request to Modify the Agreement

The party seeking the modification(s) will furnish the other party a written Notice of Request to Modify Agreement in the form of a letter from the UAW SAC Advisor to the Vice President People Systems in the case of the Union, or vice-versa in the case of Management, listing the provision(s) the party wishes to modify or cancel and/or briefly describing any new provisions it may wish to negotiate. Thereafter, the parties will meet on this request and attempt to resolve the issues using the principles of conflict resolution.

B.   Notice of Intent to Lockout or Strike

If after thirty (30) calendar days from the date the Request is received, the parties are unable to reach consensus, the initiating party for

Saturn Corporation or the UAW SAC Advisor for the Union may serve a written Notice of Intent to Lockout or Strike in the same manner as described in "A" above. Thereafter, if a satisfactory agreement is not reached after negotiations for five (5) working days from receipt of this Notice, the moving party may initiate its action.

34. RATIFICATION

Provisions for ratification and notice thereof will be provided.

COMMITMENT OF PARTIES

Saturn and the Union acknowledge that the matters set out in this memorandum are neither all inclusive nor complete. The parties acknowledge that in arriving at this Agreement, additional matters have been extensively discussed and serve as the UAW/Saturn Guiding Principles for the parties to follow in fulfilling the mission of Saturn, and in their relationships with each other. It is the intention of the parties to rely upon those principles to provide guidance for future agreements.

INTERNATIONAL UNION, UAW
UAW LOCAL 1853
UAW LOCAL 1810
SATURN CORPORATION

July 23, 1985

Mr. Alfred S. Warren, Jr.
Vice President
General Motors Corporation
General Motors Building
Detroit, Michigan 48202

Dear Mr. Warren:

This will confirm that [in] the discussions regarding the proposed
Memorandum of Agreement between Saturn Corporation and the International Union, UAW, I advised you of the following:

The UAW views Saturn as a special project designed to maintain small
car production with a high degree of domestic content in the United
States that will provide jobs having compensation and benefits which
will maintain the standard of living now enjoyed by our members.

The UAW considers the proposed Memorandum of Agreement as a
"special case" because it is specifically designed as an integral part of
the Saturn approach.

Therefore, the UAW does not consider this Memorandum of Agreement
as a precedent regarding the Union's policy at any other facility, including those at General Motors.

Sincerely,
Owen Bieber
President